# A
# Cowgirl's
# Return

**Published by:** Red Oar Press Oklahoma

**Text Design by:** Red Oar Press

**Cover Design by:** Red Oar Press

**ISBN-10:** 0-9600247-2-7

**ISBN-13:** 978-0-9600247-2-8

**Library of Congress Control Number:** 2020933069

**Distributed by:** Robin Ross

Printed and bound in USA.

# A
# Cowgirl's
# Return

*The story of survival after a traumatic brain injury*

## ROBIN ROSS

Red Oar Press

EDMOND

## Dedicated to my Parents

Mom inherently knew when to coddle me, when to push me, when to accept my disabilities; she knew when to demand accountability and always she loved me. Mom never showed anger, disappointment, nor disgraced by my altered physical appearance, my lack of correct speech or my unacceptable public behavior. My mother sheltered me from public judgment and yet she spurred me onward and drove me to return both mentally and physically. Without my mom and her loving heart, I would have failed at climbing this large mountain to recovery. A Mom's love is beyond compare; she willingly gave me her life for over ten years of hard effort and constant guidance. Dad was the strong silent man in the background that supplied for our earthly needs and he willingly shared his wife of 65 years with his adult child that had been broken. This book is dedicated to my hard working and God fearing parents who always led by example.

# In Praise Of

*"Robin Ross was determined not to adopt a victim mentality after the brain injury that changed her life forever. To those who are suffering, she says "A Christian's isn't to fix, but to offer hope through Jesus Christ. "If you are suffering or have a loved one who is, this book is for you."*

-Marion Duckworth

Marion Duckworth is a speaker, Bible teacher, lay counselor, and award-winning writer of sixteen books and hundreds of articles. A former columnist for "Power for Living "and a past president of the Oregon Christian Writers.

*"Robin is working with the families of recovering head injury patients. She has matured significantly in her recovery and is very committed to excellence in head injury recovery programs, particularly in guiding families in their support of the head injury victims."*

-Dr. Ronald E. Jutzy, MD, FAANS

*"Robin's book shares an in-the-trenches view of what a traumatic brain injury person experiences. Medical personnel can glean first-hand knowledge among these pages of what frightens and what encourages TBI individuals. Caretakers can find a double blessing of information since Robin's mom candidly shares surprising nuggets of what did and didn't help as she struggled to reclaim her daughter. And for TBI's who hopefully can read at some time, it will no doubt inspire them to continue the rocky road toward recovery. This is indeed a unique story of the complexity of an injured brain and one person's remarkable recovery."*

- Gala Nettles

Gala Nettles is an accomplished freelance writer for numerous magazines and newspapers. She has over 16 well received books in print.

## Ronald E. Jutzy, MD, F.A.A.N.S.
St. Luke's Clinic - Neurology

**RONALD E. JUTZY, M.D.**
NEUROLOGICAL SURGEON

125 E IDAHO, SUITE 102
BOISE, IDAHO 83712

TELEPHONE (208) 381-7300
FACSIMILE (208) 381-7295

May 5, 2011

RE: Robin Ross
To Whom it May Concern,

Robin Ross has been a patient of mine for many years. I met Robin as a result of a very severe closed head injury where she fell with a horse and had an acute subdural hematoma. She was in a very deep coma and had a slow and laborious climb to wellness, largely driven by her high level of motivation and good family support.

Robin is working with the families of recovering head injury patients. She has matured significantly in her recovery and is very committed to excellence in head injury recovery programs, particularly in guiding families in their support of the head injury victims.

Please assist Robin in any way that seems best and guide her to families and hospital personnel that need encouragement and support. She has a big heart and, more importantly, she has a wealth of experience in working with people in recovery.

Sincerely,

MAY 1 7 2011

Ronald E. Jutzy, MD

REJ/ak

# Table of Contents

# Introduction

Traumatic Brain Injury & A Cowgirl's Return is an inspiring self help book filled with suggestions. I am an experienced over comer of a life altering severe TBI; I am not an educated book learned expert. I know the loss, and I know the excitement of recovery. Only God knows our abilities and He blessed me to be able to write this book by myself and share my personal story.

Are you searching for HOPE to empower yourself or a loved one from the damage and stigma related to a Traumatic Brain Injury? Are you searching for Answers? Are you searching for a pathway to defeat and understand the terror and losses of living with a severely damaged and broken brain? Do you know how to reach the TBI sufferer? If you have not had a severe TBI and overcome the deficits, then you do not have the knowledge or the understanding. I have had a severe TBI; I have overcome.

This plainspoken book is written with honesty, showing the pain and the confusion that I as a TBI lived through, alongside a plan for recovery. A plan of Hope is the main focus. Every TBI is unique. I provide goals and advice based on my own experience as to what brought me home. I provide proven coping skills. My unique story includes answers to help explain the mystery road your loved one could be traveling. Are you looking for answers to manage and combat PTSD; Post Traumatic Stress Disorder. I give you the answers that helped me to heal, and I explain what gave me the necessary, powerful, enduring desire and strength to return.

As I write my personal wellness story, I want you to know as a caregiver the power is yours; you direct, and you design the recovery path for your loved one. I am not suggesting that you use the exact same path, maybe one quite different than what I chose and I hold. I am encouraging you to choose the greatest passion your loved ones enfold dear in their hearts—whatever passion you think will work to motivate them. I do hope to draw you closer to God, but it is your choice. I chose God; I will continue to choose Him every time. You may not believe in the Lord; He is my rock and my salvation. See (St. Matthew 10:32-33)

My inspiring story is for everyone; it was written for all to benefit and to help each person move toward recovery. You may find many applicable suggestions and informative truths for your loved one. I choose to give the Glory to God.

## The Accident and Information Learned

### *Fall 2017*

I am a Traumatic Brain Injury survivor. HOPE is one of the main ingredients needed to overcome. I do have HOPE to offer and to share in an often hopeless situation. Traumatic Brain Injuries are devastating. A damaged brain can cause mental and physical function to cease in a normal timely manner. Doctors voice the medical evidence and all of the negative aspects a brain injury entails. I am voicing the possibility of a return from this debilitating injury.

I want to help victims of brain injuries become survivors. As you read this book, you will see answers to questions you have possibly not yet thought of asking for you or your loved one. Think outside of the box. Keep the book handy to reference during the different stages of your loved one's recovery process. There is no proven schedule; the brain is a mystery. I beat the medical diagnosis. With hope and proper help, more people might find recovery.

## Spring 1994

I am a horse trainer. It was May 27th when I chose to load up my horses and my good dog. The day was glorious in its dawning; I felt unstoppable. I was riding great and showing to win. My business was good; my horses were better. Jessie, my loyal Rottweiler, and I had arisen at the break of morning to do the ranch chores. The horses needed breakfast before loading them in the trailer. It was a brisk, spring morning. Mist was rising off of the creek on our property. I was alive, filled with happiness and the thrill of seeking winning days ahead. Jessie felt my excitement; she bound around me like a pup. I was at the peak of my professional life. This time in my life was the most productive period for financial gain and personal success.

Thirty-seven is a fine age. I was living it large and dreaming larger. I drove my black double cab one ton dually pulling the four-horse gooseneck trailer to the Quarter Horse show in Caldwell, Idaho. I was singing and joyfully howling along with the radio as I departed the driveway of our Payette, Idaho horse training facility. I had no idea of what the day had in store.

In my horse trailer was four head of nice performance horses of varying age. Potential show horses need to be hauled and subjected to different environments. I was preparing and schooling the horses for future competitions. It was to be an easy fun day of riding and seeing my many friends. It unfolded to be a life altering and tragic day for myself, my family, and my friends.

### My Recall

I recall arriving early, getting my horses unloaded, tied safely to the trailer, and then sitting in the show office visiting with the show secretary, Eula Dunn. Next, I had coffee with my friends at the concession stand. It was a normal spring day, and life was good. I was feeling happy with my horses and confident of good things in our future. I saddled up, left Jessie with my rig, and went to work.

People later told me that I had a productive, good day of schooling my horses. It began sprinkling lightly as I trotted my last horse towards the trailer to unsaddle. My horse slipped, and I took hold to settle him. However, instead of settling, he fell hard on the wet and slick ground. I rode him down while he collapsed on his left hip and his left shoulder. I stayed astride my young horse, and when he went down, my head and my neck received a whiplash effect as it hit the solid ground with deadly force. My brain bounced around inside my skull, creating bruising and bleeding. Profuse bleeding occurred on the inside and outside of my brain, which created immense cranial pressure. Later, my neurosurgeon would describe the damage done to my brain as a comparison to a watermelon being tossed out of a window with the melon being severely damaged on contact.

By the grace of God, qualified people were there and found me lying trapped under my horse. They acted quickly, attempting to control my convulsions and blood loss. The ambulance took me to a hospital in Caldwell, Idaho in record time. Once they received me at the hospital, I was given meds to control the seizures which the bleeding on my brain was creating. This hospital stabilized me by cauterizing the blood flowing from the outside veins on my head. I was rushed onward to the trauma unit at St. Al's in

Boise, Idaho. An emergency left craniotomy was performed to relieve pressure on my brain.

The medical preoperative diagnosis was: *1) closed head injury 2) acute left epidural hematoma 3) right temporal contusion 4) right frontal intracerebral hematoma 5) right subdural hematoma over convexity and frontal tip.*

Name of Operation: *left temporal craniotomy with evacuation of epidural hematoma and coagulation of two branches of the middle meningeal artery.*

Limited summary of procedure: *entire head was shaved, an oval shaped free bone flap approximately 5 cm by 3 cm was cut out of the midtemporal skull and removed; after surgical procedure: the bone was replaced with stainless steel staples and was then scrubbed and debrided and was closed loosely with nylon interrupted sutures in a through and through fashion. Estimated blood loss during surgery—200 cc.*

The intention of this book is to provide hope and inspiration at a time that is very dark to most victims and families. I had a severe traumatic brain injury (TBI), and my Glasgow Coma Scale rating was "3". The scale ranges from a severe "1" being near vegetative, to a less damaged rating of "15". Much of my brain's hard drive was deleted. The neurosurgeon told my parents there was a 5% chance of recovery; I would probably remain in a wheelchair. He was very doubtful if my brain would heal fully and allow me to return mentally or physically to a satisfactory degree. Additionally, he told them my vision might be gone in my left eye.

In layman's terms, my brain was badly damaged, and the internal bleeding was severe. I was near death and barely holding onto my life. My future cognizant skills were altered; I was in a coma and on life support. I was fed through a tube in my belly; machines were keeping me alive. My accident and the resulting injury was violent, ugly, and severely life threatening. From this day forward my life was forever changed; lives of my parents and my family were shattered. This is not a journey one takes alone. In order to survive and recover, your family and friends become most vital.

The horse show community is a tight, close-knit, and caring industry; therefore, someone in the horse show office called to alert my mother at home. She said, "Hurry to the St. Al's Hospital in Boise. Robin had a bad accident, and her head has been smashed." Can you imagine the fear and horror this statement would have put into my mom's heart?

My mother was the main caregiver during my long recovery. She is a determined woman; she was also the fierce leader of my support group. She found no written suggestions, and no guides to help me recover; she found nothing provided by a traumatic brain injury survivor to which she could refer. My mom made up her own solid, common sense plan to help me return. As I gradually awoke and recovered, we adjusted the guide to fit what we perceived my needs to be. During my recovery, either she or I recognized what motivated and drove my mind and body to accomplish tasks and we took note.

The advancement of the medical world and doctor's skills make even more survivals possible today; however, mere survival is not satisfactory. I have a personal goal throughout this book and in sharing my story to inspire Hope and offer suggestions for other TBI survivors and their families and friends. This truth told book does bring hope and awareness to TBI survivors and the entire uninformed world—truth provided by a survivor, instead of merely a scholar.

It might sound like a simple fix to help your loved one to help him/herself; however, you need to realize that it will not be easy and for sure not simple. Read my story, and evaluate your loved one's capabilities. These suggestions are made for the caregivers, the support groups, and the person in recovery to consider and to put in play. I am stressing the importance of God and faith and a positive belief that wellness is obtainable. It takes a continuous effort; Mom led and sometimes pushed me down the path. My friends never gave up Hope on me; I did have to work hard. Others deserve as much or more credit than I do for my recovery. Your loved one will need assistance on his or her difficult road to learning a new normal. As I recovered, we tweaked and changed my guide. Apply this guide and suggestions to your person as you see fit. With my gradual awakening, we realized more of what was important and what was not important in the process; no doubt there will be variance in your journey.

My optic nerves had been damaged; my resulting vision returned images to my brain confused and often distorted. At times, I tried to carry on a conversation with the mirage of a face due to the double picture shown in my convoluted vision. I tried to have eye contact where there were no eyes. Spoons of sugar landed on the table while choosing the wrong cup of coffee in which to add sweetener. My horizons bounced, and my step was unsure. The entire world was double; this was another puzzle for me to ponder. The brain does learn to adjust, and I became comfortable and able to compensate around this vision deficit. My somewhat dyslexic brain had been managing the double vision. Nine months into my recovery, I awoke from my daily afternoon nap. Worse confusion: the optic nerves had reunited! I no longer had to make adjustments and guess which objects were real.

Now, the nerves repaired and more changes had to be overcome; thank God the brain is an amazing, wonder-filled unknown.

Due to whacking the ground, my left ear bled for months, and my hearing was diminished. My left temporomandibular joint, TMJ, was cracked and misaligned. The life threatening injury to my brain was where the doctors concentrated their efforts. I had and have residual side effects from the accident. Nerve damage had occurred in my spine. Physically, my right side was more affected even though the original blow was on the left side of my head. My right side began to atrophy, and it was weak. My right arm began to posture, and my right leg and my right foot had numbness, neuropathy, and constant pain.

My memory remains impacted, and it takes a conscious effort to retain facts. My word recall was poor, and I had an unrecognizable voice. My voice, when I found it and was able to communicate, was guttural and sounded robotic; forming sentences was beyond me. My balance and my motor skills were limited. I fell off of my bed. I would fall when trying to stand, and I could not balance on my feet. It was like the world moved and had quakes that shook only me. I could not feed myself. My sense of smell was gone. False, nasty odors would get stuck in my nose. To this day, when I go into a hospital, I imagine the odor of fecal material and decay. I could not tell what was real and what was imagined. I couldn't reason, and my thoughts were jumbled. I had lost almost all control of myself and relied upon caregivers for all of my care. My situation was surreal. For those of you reading, who are caregivers, I pray you never understand the emotional abyss or this deep feeling of despair. Don't tell your loved one, "I understand," because you do not.

Every brain injured person is not the same or even comparable; some are not aware of their state of disrepair or limitations. Luckily, I did become aware; but I was sickened by me. I attributed the label of "Brain Injury" to being less than smart. I knew I was lacking, and my mind was not functioning correctly. My conscious state and situation encouraged me to put every bit of strength and effort into recovering. I labeled myself "crazy." This was not acceptable and drove me to try and to reach a high level of recovery.

This manuscript is the heart of my return. Mom's journal showed her successful way to reach me by evaluating and making smart choices; it showed the near total devastation her love helped defeat. My awakening memoirs and the graphic Chapter titled Enlightenment make it clear that my thoughts were shattered and my previous structured life was gone.

At the beginning of the struggle, my mind was broken. It was as if the world was having a riotous party inside my brain and I was not invited. My head was heavy, full of mud and of torment. In my earliest unstable state, I did do some self-mutilation. I felt I could control this self-inflicted pain; I was lost and searching for control in any part of my life.

Today, I have a great life, but deficits do remain. No caregiver can know what disarray his or her TBI person's mental state is on any given day. The journey is going to look different for every person. Honestly evaluate, and dig deep to find the person inside the injured body. This effort might take a long while and involve much thought and work on your part. I was so tired every day. Don't expect injured persons to give you many solid answers. They are not being evasive; they probably do not know the answers, or their thoughts are too jumbled to deliver. They may very well be doing their current best to communicate.

I am not a doctor or a therapist. This is not a strict "how to" book. I am not qualified to give orders or to prescribe medication. My book is written anecdotally with truth and to give you and your loved one Hope. My story might help you navigate a clear path when things seem scattered and beyond comprehension. A person searching for guidance and answers might be pleased to find and utilize my informed writings; this is what worked for me. I didn't just read a book and decide to make myself an expert on Traumatic Brain Injury; I lived my proven message, and I am on fire to share it. Help your loved one to have the same opportunity; help them find his or her true potential and return beyond the medical prognosis.

A strong-willed family with a deep connection to God is what grounds me. Every step of every day, I am supported by loving family and friends; mine is an amazing and unique recovery, as will be every success story. Empower your loved one's effort to heal and return. I cannot state too many times that much of the success will rely on support groups and caregivers. These people need to gather information and use their own imaginations to provide the encouraging stimulus. I believe and I pray everyone can improve his or her lot in life. The final degree of recovery you or your loved one will reach is not known; there is almost always hope for improvement. Step aboard my travels, and use my story to help your loved one recover to his or her highest potential.

Be intense and be strong, as this is not an easy journey; be kind as it is a long maddening walk. Knowing that your brain is not functioning on a normal level is frustrating and demoralizing; you are repeatedly referred to as "Brain Injury". How would you like to be thought of as a person functioning with an injured brain and having a severe traumatic brain injury? Being described as broken is defeating, humiliating, and sad. I was in a deep coma for 24 days, and I do not have any true recollections of this time. My memories are littered with other peoples' stories and their recall. People often ask if I had a near death experience, and I reply, "No, I had a near God experience."

It is impossible to separate my memories or lack of memory from heard conversation and retold stories. I do not recall feeling hurt; nor was I scared while in the very deep coma. God never forsakes us; I was warm and sleeping. After I began to emerge from the coma, my pain and confusion began. As I tried to resurface, I was terrified, and the headaches were monumental. I was scared and I was lost. Telling anyone or running away was not possible. I was a prisoner in my own broken mind and disabled body.

I struggle after 20 years to say and do the correct social amenities and manage daily function. When taking care of myself physically, my body and my mind carry me through the rigors of each day. Much rest, a better diet, little-to-no alcohol, and moderation in most things helps me operate with some efficiency. Stress, either mental or physical, is my worst enemy. Post Traumatic Stress disorder haunts me.

Everyone has failure issues—scars are both seen and hidden. Consider yourself blessed by God, and do your daily best. For a long while, my emotions ran high and out of control. The gamut was exhausting. I was scared, then angry, confused and sad; then wildly, I would relive the feelings, again and again. I grieved for the loss of myself—I knew the original Robin was gone. My pituitary gland had been moved and damaged, so my hormonal changes were confused as well. These unknown, uncontrolled feelings were nearly insurmountable. Years later, as my recovery progressed, I found peace, and I recognized that a kinder, happier, and a better person had resulted from my tests and trials. I wouldn't recommend it, but as it turned out, it was not all bad. Perhaps, many of you will overcome and feel the same.

I went through a socially unacceptable time. I spoke to people with unsolicited opinions. I would interrupt and openly share my concerns for their actions. Decision was slow to form, and then I would become rock solid on my position. I was often rude, and I was often in the wrong.

As a caregiver, don't be embarrassed or too critical of your loved one in social situations; I often ventured out of this box of accepted social parameters and I probably will continue to do so. My common sense support group would guide my actions and speech to educate me as to 'okay' and 'not okay' reactions given by me; sometimes they did the lesson with laughter and chiding, but only if I was laughing as well.

For a time, spontaneous words erupted from peripheral influences. I might be outside and joining successfully in a conversation when an airplane or jet would fly overhead and enter my radar. Instead of continuing a normal sentence, I would say "Airplane" loudly once or twice then slip back to my intended subject, totally unconcerned with the interruption. Maybe, an odor would be noticeable so I would declare "Stinks!" If I saw something that I judged ugly, I would state "Ugly" in the middle of a discourse. In other situations, a refrigerator might start to quietly hum in the room, so I would unconcernedly interject the word "Refrigerator" into the flow of my speaking. I'd hear a toilet flush; out the word "Toilet" would pop. My loving concerned support group got this abstract behavior slowed and soon stopped by kindly admonishing me, yet I remained welcome within the conversation. I am fortunate to be loved and accepted; embarrassing me was never their intention.

My God given internal filter recovered, I was blessed by the return of my personal discernment.

It seems to me that I display and feel different responses and actions coming from the spectrum of Autism and or possibly a touch of the Tourette's syndrome. The brain is a mystery. If possible reach for professional help for your loved one to understand and dissuade the unwanted actions.

The "lack of control" of my own person was the most frightening. Being even temporarily crazy is hard to accept. By loss of control, I mean I was not capable, nor was I allowed to make many decisions for myself. I had no physical control and little mental clarity…   Where was the wheel chair to be parked?  What did I want to drink?  Why was I sitting tied to the toilet, and who made the decision that I needed to use the bathroom? Is it time to be awake? Is it time to sleep? Who is making these decisions, and when will my personal power return? Who turned on the radio, and why that type of music? I heard laughter. Who is laughing, and what is funny? I was just along for the ride; I understood very little of the day's events. I know that for me there are worse things and worse places to be than death. I was residing in a personal and a deep, dark, frightening Hell.

Traumatic Brain Injury people often end up warehoused in Nursing Homes; a cognitive viable person may be hidden deep inside. A TBI being blessed with a caregiver that is willing to, however long, make it his or her life's work to help restore a loved one's broken brain is possibly the key. The brain and brain stem cannot have been too damaged, as a sheared brain stem cannot be restored unless a true miracle performed by God occurs for this person. Listen to the doctors and their medical diagnoses. Yet, believe that recovery is possible until you realize it is not. Tragically, some are broken beyond repair.

As the years went and my world advanced, I began to question whether or not I should do something beyond the realm of my normal life; might I have gotten better to assist others to recover? My efforts are worth sharing if I help one person and one family find their own peace and manage to return. I ride horses, and I enjoy a fine existence. Now, I am choosing to alter my day's work. For the last twenty years there has been a chant of "Write me! Write me! Write me!" incessantly repeated in my head. I cannot rest—God has a better purpose for me and my blessed recovery.

I have accepted my new place in life. My written story needs to be told and shared. The story is pouring out of me with ease and confidence. I am positive this is the road for me. Not all of my suggestions may work for your loved one's unique injury. Read this, and apply common sense. Then, use my guidelines wisely to fit your considered case, or don't use my proven success ideas if you think they are not applicable to your loved one. Make good choices. Possibly, you already have a plan for your loved one, but consider implementing some of my suggestions.

Be aware that a Traumatic Brain Injury and the resulting issues are not caused only by a major, horrendous accident or occurrence. There are many factors to consider, not just the power or intensity of the episode. Do not laugh off a whack to the head or a severe shaking. A hard fall can shake your brain. I hear people say, "No worries, he's hard headed." Any degree of head injury is not something to take lightly. When in doubt, see a professional. Get an MRI. A brain bleed or a mini stroke can devastate. Err on the side of caution when it comes to Brain Injuries.

A severe traumatic brain injury does not play out like the movies portray. Most people don't just awake from a coma with a fully functioning mind and body. A brain injury often changes personality and perception. A severe TBI is usually a devastating event that shatters and changes a person's world, and it changes the world of everyone in his or her circle of life.

## Family Ranch Roots and Strengths

I was raised in Eastern Oregon on a high desert ranch. I knew that the weak would not survive; the sick animal that does not come to water and feed is not going to live. My people are strong people, and we are close to our Creator; I am blessed with strong genes. We believe in God, and we love our country. My family consisted of my older brother Bill, my mom, my dad, and myself. We lived quite isolated most of the year; there was over 60 miles of dirt road to get to our primary home. For seven months of the year, we were with the cattle on over 100,000 acres of federal land.

Many days, we left camp in the mornings astride a good horse traveling at a trot to tend to the cattle. We came home tired at night, and we went to bed early. Life was simple, and the available choices were few. My heritage is Agriculture with husbandry of the land and animals. I grew up with no electricity; we had no TV, no stereo, and, of course, no household running water or bathroom facilities. We had a lovely, wooden outhouse placed over 50 yards from out our back door. The only running water we had came from one of us running out to the spring, filling the bucket, quickly returning it to the kitchen counter, and replacing the long-handled, granite dipper into the fresh water for communal usage.

My background is Ranch, Rodeo, and then the Horse Competition arena. In 1950 my dad, John W. Ross, won the Northwest Championship Saddle Bronc Riding in Cheyenne, Wyoming. In 2008 he was inducted into the Buckaroo Hall of Fame in Winnemucca, Nevada. Ranch, rodeo, and near all horse people are tough survivors who are not afraid of work; nor do they shy away from strife. A fellow member attempting to return from an injury, illness, or ill fate back to the world of horses can count on united support. Loyalty is a trait shared among this empathetic group.

The horse is a strong facilitator. I had to get my good life back and return to the work, which included horses. Nothing else was acceptable. Quality and not quantity of life is what matters. The power of positive thought and positive visualization are two main ingredients in the recipe of wellness. Take the time to remember what passion existed in your injured loved one's life prior to the devastation. Help your loved one to regain the idea of it, and encourage him or her to search out that lost passion. Ask leading, easy questions to help your loved one's recall of successes and fun. Remember to wait for whatever time is necessary for your loved one to ponder on it. Allow your loved one to become a player in the game to remember and to actively rejoin life. The idea is to make your loved one proud of his or her past. Encourage your loved one to find the desire to return with strength and a feeling of earned accomplishment.

## My Advice from Information Gathered

Give it thought, and try your ideas. Rethink and try again; you might find the golden key. Your loved one will probably need a totally different dream and goal than mine. Recovery from any life altering illness or injury takes an inherent, personal hardiness. An inherent, personal hardiness means that you are strong-minded and driven. It takes a strong spirituality. Love and guidance from others does speed us down the road to wellness. I say speed, but probably this trek is going to be a long, arduous one.

My neurosurgeon told me, "He, himself, like everyone else,

was getting older every day." He said, "In my case, I was blessed to be recovering every single day, and my journey could last and improve for years." Look forward to the positive changes and growth. Give your loved one time, and always applaud the positive changes. You can't know how hard your loved one is trying or the effort each action takes. Don't show pity, disgust, or anger in your expression or your voice. You might be the one person who is keeping your loved one anchored. Don't doubt your importance, and don't weaken in the challenges ahead.

My near-month comatose stay at the St. Alphonsus Hospital in Boise, Idaho was the first step. Next, I went on to the Idaho Elks' Rehabilitation Hospital for over an additional month. The early prognosis was that I would remain in the therapy rehabilitation facility for at the very least six months; I proved them wrong. I defied many of the medical limitations; I wanted my good life back. I had to relearn hand to eye coordination, relearn my speech, occupational skills, and mental skills. I had intense physical and mental rehab. My center of balance was gone. I was kept tied in my bed and tied on chairs and toilets. With help, time, and determination, I advanced from supine, to a wheelchair, to a belly band held by a support person, to a walker, then cane, and finally back to my own two shaky legs with my right side remaining weaker.

Dr. Ronald E. Jutzy is a great neurosurgeon and a caring God filled man. I received excellent rehab care, and I was given a good start. We (my mother and I) used any and all suggestions to the positive. A placebo works if you think it works; consider different options before turning aside. Water Therapy and ice gave my headaches and my confusion the best quick fix. Swimming and showering with the water cascading softly over my broken head provided calming coolness. We used homeopathic treatments, acupuncture, massage, and chiropractor adjustments. We grasped and tried any other assistance available. No sensible suggestion was overlooked.

An unconventional doctor gave me a $10,000 trip to Cancun, Mexico. I was their first brain and spinal injury. They treated me there with natural ingredients applied onto my skin with the Feckler Response. Supposedly, they used only plants grown on the Yucatan Peninsula. Dr. Vigil later served time in prison for misrepresentation. He had no medical credentials recognized in the United States.

Years after the treatment, I was subpoenaed by the FBI and flown to Boise from my Oklahoma home. I testified at the Grand Jury. Dr. Vigil had helped me, and his acupuncture treatments gave me pain relief. I did gain better function of movement and mental clarity under his care. I was saddened by his imprisonment. Dr. Vigil supplied something that helped my confidence and gave me back my center of balance. Possibly his faith in my recovery helped my psyche to believe it was true. Who really knows? I believe my faith in the Lord assisted me at every turn.

I have been blessed with acquiring the best of people as friends in my lifetime. Dr. James Kranz, a successful chiropractor in Boise, Idaho, supplied me with Brain Sustain. It is a nutritional supplement, heavy on Vitamin B. I continue to take it daily. The Brain Sustain seems to keep me on an even emotional keel. Dr. Kranz gave me chiropractic treatments and offered positive opinion and his friendship. Ten years after my accident, he introduced me to one of his valued friends and associates, Jim Hollingsworth.

Dr. James Hollingsworth is a Chiropractor. He is also a successful Hypnotherapist and Sports Coach in Boise, Idaho. We have never met face to face, but we have spent hours talking on our cell phones. He personalized positive impact CDs for me. I can close my eyes and hear his voice and recall his mental exercises. His soothing voice and visualizations helped me envision recovery. Good people are available and will assist you if you approach them with respect and with a contagious hope of recovery.

Most people want to see success and happiness. I did not credit nor mention everyone that played a role in my recovery; God puts the people we need in our lives when we need them. Barbra Schulte, a talented horsewoman and clinician, has created a Mentally Tough program. I did not know Barbra, but I was familiar with her success story and her many accomplishments. Barbra heard my story and blessed me by sending me her tapes and workbooks, and we have visited by phone. During self-conscious, fearful, long-lasting periods of weakness, I hungered for and believed other peoples' opinions. Thank God, Mom sheltered me from bullies, and I was blessed by people willing to share their strength and put forth the impression that they felt strength was still in me to be found and to utilize.

In my journey, I have realized that many people don't consider the services of a good chiropractor as valid; massage offers relief as well. Often, medical professionals ignore the tremendous value of having your body aligned so it can operate as a well functioning machine; logically, all parts affect the whole entity. After eleven years of suffering and ignoring the misalignments and chronic crippling pain in my neck and back, we were blessed by locating and having the opportunity to be treated by Dr. Scott Wood, a chiropractor in Tishomingo, Oklahoma. Scott's knowledgeable chiropractic efforts and his treasured friendship lifted me up and relieved my pain.

Ask your oldest family friends to become involved, as they know the original you. Trudy Wilcox, a family childhood friend, made a huge contribution of her time and of her common sense, and she knew the old me well. She knew when to push and when to have compassion. For example, one follow up road trip to the Boise neurosurgeon, I could not make a decision in order to answer her simple question. Trudy had inquired, "Do you want a specialty coffee or ice cream when we go by the town of Caldwell, Idaho?" I just could not quit wavering back and forth between coffee and the choice of ice cream. Slowly, Trudy pulled to the side of the freeway by the exit ramp and sat patiently until I finally made a decision and yelled out an answer. It worked. We enjoyed ice cream! Decision making and word recall under pressure remains hard for me and it might be hard for your loved one, too. When I over think and feel pressured, my thought process slows, but it kicks in if I relax and wait for the answer to slip into my mind.

When you were a child, did you have a black magic 8-Ball that you could question, shake, wait, and the answer would slowly and magically appear in a window-like space at the top of the 8-Ball? My mind works in that manner. If I pause, then relax and quit blocking my brain synapses with anger, panic, or feelings of stupidity, the answer will usually float to the top.

Our brain is the least known part of us; it is an amazing computer and programming system. I am over

62 years old and I take no prescribed drugs at this time; I am not encouraging the stoppage of any prescribed meds. I encourage people to try everything positive. Consider all types of medical care, but do exercise caution. Predators are out there actively working to gain from another person's desperation. Realize that possibly some injuries are too devastatingly severe to overcome no matter the effort or the caregiver's sacrifices.

The major turning point for me came after months of work. The seemingly small act of getting back on a horse reconnected me with my life. Look for your loved one's deepest desire, and supply that driving force. Maybe there is a NARHA (North American Rider's Handicap Association) in your area. They have huge success. Riding a horse is as close to human travel as we can get while not actually moving our own two legs.

One day at home on our Payette, Idaho horse training facility, Dad saddled Norman. This bay gelding was a solid and dependable saddle horse. He and my mother helped me to mount. Soon, I sat astride a horse, one parent walking on each side. Slowly we rode on. How can I describe my feelings of joy and freedom? With Norman's cadence, I felt it was me who was successfully striding along. I was back in my realm. Once again, I was using my body and my mind. I was enjoying the physical and mental exercise. I was outside, aboard a horse, getting dirty, feeling fine, and visualizing success. I was so very proud of myself!

Visualization does work. Draw pictures with words to help your person dream. Make your loved one feel and smell the event you are describing. Help your loved one to crave this dream deep in his or her soul.

A severe traumatic brain injury is an ongoing recovery. If and when I tire, I become markedly less competent in most all ways. An abundant amount of sleep is required for me to function both mentally and physically. With rest, I can accomplish successfully some degree of whatsoever I believe I can accomplish. I have wanted to reach out and offer my story to help others travel the same road, but I have been hesitant; it does pull me back to remember and allow the feelings of the deep crippling confusion and the loss. In this book, I am being a truth teller with Hope that you might have more compassion for all TBI's and their struggles. Remember that, but for the grace of God go you. Most people fixate on what they cannot do instead of rejoicing and embracing what they can master.

At the beginning, my confidence was zilch. I was terribly disorientated, confused, scared, and limited in nearly all ways. Your brain does control each body function, thought and motor skill. My brain was damaged. With most severe brain injuries, your mental processes are very confused, and your cognitive skills lessened. Compare the injury to your computer hard drive being wiped near clean or the hard drive damaged. Not a good thing for your business, right?

Even though very damaged as I came out of the coma, I was desperate to survive and be accepted back as a valuable member of the human race. I was able to and I chose to perform; I was sly and became a character actor. I could portray and strive to be whomever and whatever was expected of me for a limited time. I tried to reach other people's expectations. At moments, I could find my large vocabulary and sense of humor only to sink to near mute and stuck in mental neutral again after my room cleared of visitors. I had to regain my confidence and desire to be a capable woman, as this was the only option. Finding my new self was very frightening, and I was adrift. No one knew nor recognized how bad I was at this time—no one. I managed to hide much. It was embarrassing and disgusting to be me.

In the telling of my story, I want people to understand how confused and deceitful their loved one might be. I felt it the only way to survive, and it is how I played out the scenario—the will to live is huge. Always remember, this person had a brain injury, and remember the brain rules all.

After more than twenty years of recovery time, my confidence level is high. Now, drat, like everyone, I am getting older. But still, I feel any reasonable goal is attainable for me while not neglecting proper personal needs of rest, exercise, and good nutrition. My biggest enemies are stress, mental fatigue, and physical fatigue. Mostly, as long as I pace myself and eat and drink properly, I can perform well in everyday life. I was tested after the injury, and my IQ is 136. I can think, but often, I analyze too much. I still act with compunction, and it's hard to let go of a decision after I have it made. I remain a work in progress. My extra weight hinders my balance and my physical stamina; help your loved one to maintain a healthy body.

I have PTSD, Post Traumatic Stress Disorder, and I feel guilty for surviving. Guilt is painful and hindering, yet it is near impossible to remove this honest emotion from the minds of many survivors. If you have not walked in that person's shoes and lived his or her experiences, then how can you judge or know the devastation and guilt for remaining alive that many survivors feel? I have a Service Dog, Huckleberry Hound, who I love very much. He provides me emotional support and strength. Everyone needs someone to love and someone from whom to receive abundant love. A pet or a Service Animal gives the owner a reason to get up—the responsibility to care for a special friend. Unconditional love and loyalty is valued by us all. As a caregiver, make the most of your loved one's service animal, and let it do its work.

I've found studies that do reflect that the higher IQ people may more likely understand and find the will to fight and recover as the best option. They might realize faster that they must put out the effort to get well or this same high IQ individual may lack the common sense and discernment of a solidly grounded person; I don't think anyone truly knows. A caregiver cannot raise anyone's IQ, but a caregiver can take the time to help a loved one see the necessity of recovery in order to regain his or her good life. Not everyone has a good life to regain, so improve your loved one's home life if possible. In my opinion, it falls back in the caregiver's lap to provide the right stimuli. I repeat often and want you to understand that I credit and give much responsibility to the leader of the support team. Never ever doubt your value. If I were alone and unloved, I would have never recovered.

I continue to struggle, but when I remember to put my fears and doubts in God's hands, I can let it go and believe I am as I should be. I am fine, and I have my purpose in life, again. I know not everyone is a believer, and as a caregiver, you have to search and find the best anchor to provide encouragement to your loved one to help him or her dig deep within and keep struggling to return to the surface.

Most things came easy for me before the accident—I had a near photographic memory, I was intelligent, and I had a fair amount of athletic talent. After the injury, life became much more challenging. Putting my pants on in the morning is a balancing act and hard. I dread that simple, humbling experience every time I dress. Now, I do have much more empathy and understanding for others. Being knocked down physically and mentally can certainly open your eyes to uncontrolled and unwelcome failure. Failure tends to make us all angry. In order to combat that negative emotion, you might put effort into being nicer; nice is good, right? You will like yourself better, and your kind gestures will make the next person's entire day better. Give it a go. Just "be" and be happy. Life is choices; try to make good ones.

Parts of my personality did change with the head injury. Often, I am fearful and anxious. What does remain as a characteristic is that I am still an over achiever and a show off. But, my overall outlook on life has been altered. Prior to the injury, I felt indestructible, strong, and brave.

Now, I am fearful, I show lack of decision, and I am scared of the unknown. Sometimes, I lose control of my social skills, and I am much more easily agitated. I hate that I get loud and that I might use inappropriate cuss words. My personal preferences have changed. Prior to the injury, I had tunes playing on the radio whenever I had the option. After the injury and the confusion of too much to process, I often prefer quiet. Outside influences didn't bother me, but after the accident, I find that the constant motion of ceiling fans upset and throw me off center, and the sounds of a TV playing or a person chatting away on a cell phone gets into my head so that I cannot successfully filter the noise. Sometimes, it feels like the earth moves under my feet, and I experience a private earthquake that hits only me. The movement of fluorescent lights and their pixels dancing before my eyes makes my stomach sick. Crowds scare me, and I feel my space being invaded. Party voices and conversations tend to overload my system with stimulus that I can't handle nor comprehend, and my world becomes exhausting.

As a caregiver, keep your loved one sheltered from public scrutiny until he or she is capable of not being overcome and downtrodden. People think they are giving you a treat by pushing your wheelchair off course or by exposing your damaged self into scrutiny from the public. Remember, well meaning exposure is still exposure, and maybe your loved one does not desire to be seen as a shadow of his or her old self. Stop and consider how you would honestly feel in your loved one's position, appearance and state of health. Keep your loved one home. Let your loved one heal.

Allow your loved one to make his or her decisions about when to reappear publicly. With you, I am sharing my own weaknesses. I want to make it plain that I do not allow my deficits to stop me from enjoying life, but my mom was smart and kept me sheltered until she felt I was ready to take each step. We have not one picture of me during the worst years of my return from the injury. My positive support group held the attitude that my bad stages were only temporary so there would be no recordings or pictures taken!

I have no patience with whiners. Most people have the option to quit whining and fix the problem. For example, obese people often have pain in their joints and need surgery. Duh, losing weight and treating their bodies with respect would be a wise effort. There are many things about people and their lack of drive that upsets me. For a long time, I spoke out and offered my unsolicited and unappreciated opinions. Finally, I can keep quiet. I warn you though, don't ask me if you don't want my honest (and sometimes harsh) thoughts and suggestions.

My friends, my family, and my support group gave me the positive strength to return. They were not negative or pessimistic; surely they got tired of me talking constantly about my health. Believe that you as a caregiver are going to tire of the indecision and the repeated failures. Never did I see Mom yawn or look disgusted. She must have been near implosion, often. I was self-centered, and I felt the world revolved around me and my issues. These people managed somehow to help me see near full recovery as the only acceptable option. If Mom thought I could manage, I figured she was right, so I kept trying until I succeeded to an acceptable degree.

I had successfully competed in a tough venue before the accident. I was and I am a National Reined Cow Horse enthusiast and a proven Champion. The people involved in any competitive arena believe in winning both at the show and at their home. Their support and strength made me strong. My mother, especially, kept providing the proper stimulus to encourage me to strive to heal both mentally and physically. I borrowed other people's strength. I rode on their toughness and their encouragement. They helped me to dig deep and to overcome the sense of failure and loss. Instead of focusing and commiserating on your loved one's losses, you should embrace and celebrate their successes, be they large or small.

Honestly, I am still having problems focusing on life and living successfully in its competitive structure. We are what we think we are; therefore, I am having trouble discarding the image of myself as brain damaged. Thankfully, my injury was one that did allow for recovery. Although, being labeled and described as having a Traumatic Brain Injury causes me to feel retarded and less than capable if I allow negative thoughts to invade my mind. We all find confidence in knowing we have a good functioning brain. We feel lacking and incompetent if we have been told and know our brain is injured and failing us in any manner.

My life is not totally recovered, but I am getting

there. In retrospect, this story sounds like a Cinderella staged event. And in ways it has been, but in others it has been horridly hard and devastating. No one has a continuously paved road upon which to tread. It is a fact that not every accident, injury, or illness can be overcome. Sadly, some loved ones cannot be fixed.

My future plans are to seize the moment and appreciate the good world and good times in which we live. Horses and dogs will always be a part of my life and a major reason to get up in the morning. I would like to help others see a light at the end of their travels. I do have insight that only being disabled could teach. I am not merely book or scholastically educated; I have been taught by living and surviving the experience of a severe Traumatic Brain Injury. Please let me assist you or your loved one!

I have been successfully yet fearfully living and competing since the accident. No doubt that life is and can be frightening. I have not been enjoying the competition nor reaching my full capabilities. I am afraid, and a fear of getting hurt remains; a big fear lives within me as to the possibility of another severe painful head injury. I was like a reed in a whirlwind for quite some time.

Now, I have an insatiable need to be the master of my destiny and self at all times, and this can be very restrictive. I have to get over it. In the final call here on Earth, it is in my hands, alone, to have faith and struggle onward. I believe completely in the power of Jesus Christ and his love for us. I'm sure we all need to open our hearts to Christ and believe. I am not declaring that non-believers won't get well; I am sharing my own testimony and my own road to wellness. This strong belief is what I cling to and hold close. Choose whatever works for you and your loved one, but choose something powerful.

I had a brain injury; I am not a Brain Injury. Throughout the rest of my life, I will carry the mental baggage and history of the incident. Some days, I mourn the loss of the vanished, capable person that I am told was me. The Robin Ross that existed prior to my accident is dead and gone. Then I remember joyfully to celebrate who I am and all that remains ahead.

My world-renowned neurosurgeon declares me one of his highest level injuries that he saw return to good mental clarity and capable physical abilities. I survived, and I have recall. I can put my thoughts and my words together in legible sentences. I am the voice of the speechless, and I am being heard. Family members, support groups, and caregivers need assistance and realistic goals. A guideline and a reasonable Hope filled plan must be sought and formed.

My family totally dedicated themselves in helping me find wellness. The entire family dynamics will change when a Traumatic Brain Injury strikes; everyone needs to pull for the damaged loved one. In the midst of the tiresome work of the fray, be sure not to lose younger or older family members through the cracks of your time and efforts. Everyone is equally important, and they need your time and your love. My parents used their limited finances, common sense, and their love to find me. I was and I am blessed. We are all on a long, continuous trek of everyday survival.

Having survived a Brain Injury and then happily having returned to near normalcy gives me a totally different view and understanding. The brain injured person is not going to recover on his or her own; a traumatic brain injury does disable clear thinking and one's mobility. It probably will be a slow process and a hard accomplished, long-term job. Never doubt that your loved one needs your love and support. Reach out, take hold, and help your loved one heal.

## My Mother's Hospital Journal
By Vea Loy Ross

This section is included to provide intimate and raw insight to family members and loved one's emotions and inspiration. Remember, this section is my caregiver's experience, which may be considerably different from the next person's. Although, this approach definitely worked for us. We are offering my Mom's hospital experience to give insight and to help everyone involved cope and to provide the possibility of hope. The main caregiver is the big player. In my opinion, the caregiver has the magic wand. If used wisely and if the injured person is not damaged beyond repair, with God's help, a miracle can be done. My mother was the one who orchestrated with and held the wand. She led and she pushed me to return. It was the only option. Mom and Dad were always a team. John and Vea Loy were married for over 65 years, but this was Vea Loy's show to successfully command.

Mom could not locate any related books written by a TBI survivor; my book can provide clarity while including hope. She was searching for answers and an understanding of what might be yet to come. Wouldn't it be wonderful to know what is possibly going on in the tormented injured brain as it heals? A mother's love may be the strongest love of all. My Mom is a stout Christian woman who never doubted that I was going to return.

**Mom's Journal beginning at home in Payette, Idaho on our horse-training ranch.**

I was home alone, waiting for Robin to call and say she was coming home from the Quarter Horse Show. She wasn't showing at this event. She was getting her young horses out and about; I wasn't worried, but I did wonder why she didn't call me? Not in my wildest dreams, did I think what was about to unfold could ever happen. Her dad, John, was at the Bishop Ranch, west of Vale, Oregon for the day; he was shoeing their saddle horses. At exactly 11:57 a.m., May 27, 1994, the phone rang. Finally, I thought; it's is about time Robin checked in with me. I did not recognize the voice calling on the phone. The voice was strange and leaning towards frantic. In this same voice the woman said, "Mrs. Ross. . . Robin has been hurt." I asked how seriously?" The voice rang out, "Well, her head got smashed!"

I felt so many different things; I felt fear, non-belief, and then terror! I hung up, and I called John at Bishop's but there was no answer. I called again and again until Johnny Bishop picked up and said, "He would drive John to the Caldwell, Idaho Hospital." The phone rang, again! It was the same stricken voice telling me, "Robin was much worse than they first thought. They must use the Life Flight ambulance to fly to The Trauma Unit at St. Alphonsus Hospital in Boise, Idaho. I hung up, called Bishop's again and told them to go on to Boise! Now, I was wild with upset. What to do? I need help!

I called our niece, Linda Ross. She was in my yard within minutes to take me to Robin. Linda owned and operated a classy beauty shop in Ontario, Oregon. At the time I never even thought, but I wonder how many ladies she left in her chairs with hair undone and forgotten. When I called her, she was a blessing and she quickly came.

The drive to Boise was about 65 miles. It seemed it took us hours. As it was, we beat Robin there! The Life Flight Helicopter had broken down, so they rushed with her in an ambulance. First, they took the necessary minutes to stop at the Caldwell Hospital to stabilize her by cauterizing and stopping the external bleeding.

### Boise, Idaho / St. Alphonsus Hospital

After arriving at the hospital, Linda helped me find my way to the Emergency Room receptionist to tell her, "I am Robin Ross's mother and yes, we have insurance, Blue Shield of Idaho." We were told to sit and wait; the first of many times waiting.

Linda and I were left setting in a quiet room when suddenly beside me appeared a cute little blond named Dianne Deal. If you ever watched Touched by An Angel on TV you can understand what she grew to mean to me and Robin over the next few weeks. Dianne is Robin's friend and she is my friend, forever. Dianne was committed to Robin becoming well, and she had a big part in Rob's recovery.

Soon a very brisk, efficient man in a huge hurry burst into the room and said, "Mrs. Ross?" I said, "Yes, Robin's mom." He shook my hand and he was already going out the door as he said, "She's here. I should have you sign a bunch of papers but I don't have time and I'll see you." And then he was gone. This was Dr. Ronald E. Jutzy, her brain surgeon; with God's guidance and mercy, this good man gave us back Robin.

We were sent to a waiting room right outside of ICU. Our friend, Johnny Bishop had arrived with John, and they were waiting for us. I had never ever seen my John look so afraid. I don't remember much about waiting; I do recall the nurse saying, "Don't expect much, Mrs. Ross, she's bad," as she walked away and out of the ER Waiting Room.

I thought, "OK, but you don't know nothing, just wait, I'll go see her and you will be wrong!"

After a while the head nurse came after us—just John and I could go in. I noticed she kept looking back like I wonder how this not-too-young couple will react, when they see Robin for the first time.

At the first sight of Robin my heart froze, next I thought, "Fine, so what if she is bluish gray, her head fully wrapped, not round but sort of oblong and blood coming from one side of the bandage. Pipes, tubes, machines that made slurping noises were going on and on, but in a minute she will open her eyes and be okay. I know she will."

Only now Robin began to fight, to fight terrible, she was fighting wild and so strong. It took several men to subdue her and tie her feet and legs, also a chest vest to hold her even tighter. Pillows were put around her head as she threw it from side to side. Oh, God, what if she damages her head again? After a while, Robin was left alone with just us while the nurses observed very closely from the front desk and from Robin's monitors.

So I talked and talked to her, but she just wouldn't listen. She will though, very soon. She has to be fine, as Robin always helps me. She's the leader and she is the strong one. I need her so badly to return to tell me what to do.

"Come on, Rob, open your eyes and please stop the awful animal like noises you're making as you struggle to get loose."

I asked, "Dr. Jutzy why is she fighting like that?" He said, "I don't know, unless she thinks she is still under the horse."

"Please Rob, open your eyes – Okay, No! No!" She opened them but they looked terrified and fearfully crazed with way too much white showing in them and even worse her eyes were rolled way up in her head. "Rob, Rob, you're okay," I cried. John remained silent and stoic. He was always the strong quiet unemotional man who silently believed every trial could be beaten.

She fought on until somehow the night came and went. John returned home to care for the animals. He did come back daily to stand by my side.

The next a.m. there was no change, but at least, no worse. Medical personnel checked her often. They pounded blue gook into a hose that went straight into her stomach to feed her. The machines kept going. I hated those noisy repetitive things but I knew she had to have them and still she fought and she struggled with inner terrors.

Mietta, my great-niece, came and brought a radio. I asked if we could play it for Rob. The nurse said, "Sure," she may as well have said to me, "Do whatever; she is not going to respond."

Well, for the first of many times, we proved them wrong—

At first, I thought it was just more babbling noises, then I realized, Robin was saying something, "#@#$@#@. Two, five, no, not two, was it even five?" She said nine ...two...three?" She repeated it over and over if that was what she said, if she was saying anything at all. Then Mietta said, "Oh, my! We have the radio on the wrong station, she is requesting 92.3. I adjusted the radio; she settled down and never said one more mass of numbers.

"By Lord, she is in there, of course she is. . . I knew it all the time." The next day the radio played softly all day and she never uttered a word or number.

So I began continually repeating, "Robin, Robin, just

say one word, let me know you are hearing me and that you know we are here; we are here and loving you. Answer me, please answer me!"

All at once a voice, a voice that sounded like a tiny little person away down in a deep well, said very plain, "I love you mama." She said it only once, no more. Robin had never as an adult called me mama. I didn't care what she called me as long as she was responding. Now, who was that poor little lost-sounding person and why did she go back into silent mode? The nurses and doctor did not believe she spoke to me. They said it was not possible, but I heard her. She did speak to me. Tomorrow, Robin will open her pretty green eyes and smile; never mind that her left eye droops downward and her mouth is crooked; she will stop wildly fighting. Robin will be just fine tomorrow then better every day thereafter.

In the Traumatic Brain Injury ICU at night they wouldn't let Mietta and me stay in Robin's room. The second night we slept in very hard chairs just outside the room, but I felt like I was a million miles from her. The third night Mietta brought a pillow and blanket, which we shared while we hid in a janitor closet on the same floor. The nursing staff would have removed us if we had been found. Their reason for full eviction was overcrowding in the waiting room; the numbers had gotten so great that no one was allowed to remain at night. The janitor found us one morning; he got a shock when he opened the door and there hid two women. Not a word was said as he quietly shut the opening. The minute the ICU would let me inside, I was up and back beside her.

After three days in the Traumatic Brain Injury ICU, she remained comatose, but stable and could be moved out of there and into a guarded TBI unit. I was so glad. After they moved her with most all of her machines and her paraphernalia right next to the Nurse's Station, they moved a cot into her room for me. "Now, just watch us. Robin will wake up, and she will stop fighting. Robin will be herself and not speak with the strange tiny little person's voice from somewhere in such a lost sounding and heart breaking voice; if not today, for sure, tomorrow!"

Dianne came every day. I don't think I could have held up if not for her love, her concern, and her strength.

The first day Robin had lots of company and more phone calls. In the guarded TBI Unit, she had 80 inquiries in 24 hours. There was soon a sign placed on her door denying access without approval. We were asked to stop the phone calls. How do you tell your concerned friends and family not to call? Our good friend, Rusty Rumberger said, "I'll have the calls diverted to my phone." She kept current updates on her service, which recited the date, the time, and

Robin's daily condition.

So many wonderful friends and family were there for us. They all did everything they could, but Robin still was only semiconscious and fighting, fighting so hard.

Once I heard her say, "Oh, oh, help." I jumped up, and I found she had the catheter pulled so tight it was hurting her terribly. I had to unhook the container from the bed and dislodge the tangled hose from her body to release the pressure. Robin said, "Oh, man, having an abortion isn't what it's cracked up to be." Hey! There she is, she's back. No, no, it was just another glimpse of her, but not really. Where did that smart aleck crack come from about an abortion and was she trying to be funny or was she serious and alarmed? No more speech followed.

Robin was still fighting, still keeping her wild weird eyes closed. I was so sure she would be here by now—
I was so tired, so very tired. I went back to my cot. It seemed a waste of time as I hardly even lay down before she started to fight and struggle so hard that I had to rush back beside her. Mietta was sleeping beside me on the floor.

The next day there was not much change, lots of calls and lots of people, many beautiful flowers, teddy bears, candy, cookies, cards, and get-well banners. People coming and going, but it didn't seem to affect Robin. Nothing showed on her screens or on the blipping of her monitors;

nor did anything or any sounds appear to openly get her attention.

People reacted differently when they saw her laying there, with no long red hair left shining on her head; she was there, but not there. The men showed more emotion than the women. Often they had to leave the room to pull themselves together and some did not return until another day. At this time, her appearance and her prognosis seemed heartbreaking and bleak. The nurses told me later that two older people had come at different times and on different multiple days to Robin's hospital room door to stand and pray without ever making me aware of their visits; intercessory prayer is powerful and was much appreciated. I thought of all the wonderful family and friends who kept calling and coming to offer support and love. Our granddaughters, Cheyenne and Sabrina, and Laura, their mother, plus Bill, our son, with his wife, Cindy, was there too.

Robin's Dad was a poor driver in traffic, yet he came every day. He was quiet and seldom stayed over an hour then he drove the hour and a half home to the ranch. He always said, "I love you both and I am sure she will be fine."

A distant family member came one day as I was standing outside the Unit. He looked at me and said, "Man, are you having a bad hair day!" Having a bad hair day? Are you for real? Me? Do I have hair? I have more important things to think about than my hair. Although, as a rule I am aware of how I look. I do like to look nice so after the smart aleck departed, I took my purse which only had a very hairy perfume tasting toothbrush in it and some lipstick and I went to the restroom. I stepped inside the door to the sink and mirror.

I glanced up and saw this tired, messy, old lady standing behind me, waiting to use the sink. I said, "Excuse me," and moved to one side—to my horror, she moved too! This old rumpled lady was me! Wow. Maybe those people were right. "Go home and rest," they kept saying. "She will need you more, later." So I did drive home that evening, but I turned around and went right back after I showered, washed my hair and got more clothes. I decided this separation will not do and I belong with Robin now and later, too! Back to the hospital, I went that evening to be with Rob. She needed me!

My mom and my sister, June, came over. June brought a bunch of roses from her garden with one exceptionally pretty big, red rose in the bouquet. I thought, "As long as that rose stays so bright and strong, everything will be okay."

The other roses faded and fell apart. This one special rose still looked fine, or so I told myself. I held onto it for several days, and people would say, "Let's throw that sorry looking rose away." My answer was, "No! No! It is fine. Leave it alone." One day, I awoke to find some extra efficient person had taken the rose and thrown it away! They had even washed and returned the empty vase onto the counter. I quickly rolled over to see if Robin was still okay. She was and even though the rose was gone, I knew it had done its job!

I was very tired, so I readied myself to go to my cot to sleep; it had been a long day. There was not much change in Robin; she was still fighting to be loose. I helped with her daily normal hygiene. This day, as I was brushing her teeth, she surprised me and quickly grabbed the brush from my hand. She had not made coordinated movement any time prior. This evening, she brushed her teeth like a woman possessed. She made her gums bleed and could have nearly knocked her tonsils down her throat. I wrestled the toothbrush away, and believe me, I never tried that again; nor did I tell the nurses what had occurred. I doubt they would have believed she was capable of the speedy movements and quick reflexes, and they would have thought me confused and unreliable.

We were at a critical point, and I was at a loss; Robin was failing and I agonized. I cannot do this alone. There it is—The Answer—I can't do it alone and I am never alone. I am not alone; I will ask God to intercede and guide us. "Please, God, help me." I remembered, long ago, I had to admit that I couldn't do without The Lord's help. Robin's dad had osteomyelitis, and a below the knee amputation was done while he was also fighting Spinal Meningitis in 1962. The doctor at the Veteran's Hospital said, "John most likely will not survive from complications considering his poor state of health going into surgery." I remembered then I was just as I am now—in bed and so scared and alone. Now, I knew exactly what to do. It worked the first time—so simple, so easy, what took me so long?

When the hospital was all quiet for the night and Robin was still for a moment, I prayed, "God, help me, I can't do it alone." Then I slept for a while. Robin awoke me during the night; once again, she was restless and thrashing. I felt the need to talk in a strong, sure, authoritative voice to her.

"Robin, Robin, listen to me." She seemed to quiet down. I sensed she was listening.

I said, "You are tired, so very tired. We are at a Quarter Horse show. Your horse fell and hurt your head, but you are okay. Do you hear me? You are out from under him." "Come on. Let's load up all four of the horses you have here. We have them all in the trailer. Get your dog, Jessie. Rob, since your head hurts, I'll drive, and you rest. Just rest, no, no, don't fidget, just sit beside me in the pickup and rest."

Robin was very still in the hospital bed, listening for me to go on. I talked on and on about each place and bend in the road, as we each knew it well. She stayed quiet and flat in her hospital bed as she listened and seemed to be riding along with me as I talked.

"We are turning into our ranch drive," I said. "We are home. Come on, I'll help you put the horses in their stalls and feed them. Also, let's do all the other chores." I named each and every animal on the place, horses, dogs, cats, etc. Finally I said, "Now, let's cross the creek bridge and go into your house, watch that step, I'll flip on the light, very good, go ahead and undress then I'll help you into the shower since you might still be a bit sore."

All of a sudden I thought, "My God" I have her in my power. I looked at her, and for the first time she looked so peaceful. She was breathing soft and slowly as she lay in her bed; I can't stop now. I couldn't do it alone; miraculously I knew I wasn't alone in the room. "Please God, don't stop, now."

I continued, "Into the shower you go, Robin. Oh, that so-and-so creaking shower door, we've got to fix that. Be careful don't bump your head, I know and I am sorry as it must hurt. The cool shower will feel so wonderful. I'll wait just outside the door for you. Are you done?"

No answer. I repeated, "Robin, are you done showering?" In a voice I could begin to barely recognize she said, "No, I gotta wash my hair." Her hair!? She doesn't have any hair!

I thought again of the first time I had seen her broken head unwrapped. I refused to dwell on that ugly memory.

Instead, I said, "Take your time; go ahead and wash your hair—there, it looks fine. Dry yourself off and put on your big old sloppy blue housecoat that you love. Now, Robin, let's go sit you down in your pretty new comfortable recliner. Come on, let me help you. There, let's put up the footrest, okay now, relax. There that feels so very good. You are all done for the night! You are home, so rest, Robin. Mom's here with you. Please sleep, Robin, sleep."

She slept—quiet and smooth, no fighting, no thrashing. She rested, and she never did fight out of control, again. "Thank you God!"

Morning came, and I was right there to reassure her. "Yes, she had been hurt by a horse, but now she was safe and she was healing in the hospital. Yes, I understood her head hurt terribly. Now, she would be fine and all was being taken care of at the ranch so she needed to recover and be herself." Things just went on from there. I, by God's guidance, had done very good work by talking her down and bringing her home. Robin was able to move on towards recovery.

*End of Mom's Recorded Hospital Journal*

## My First Memories and Awakening

I remained in the Boise, Idaho Saint Alphonsus Hospital in a coma for over three weeks. I was monitored in the Critical Care Brain Injury Unit for days. After my being stabilized, I was kept an additional amount of days on the Head Injury Floor in the Traumatic Brain Injury Guarded Unit.

Next, I was moved to the Idaho Elk's Rehabilitation facility in Boise, Idaho. The Elk's and their trained therapists played a powerful, positive role in my recovery.

An untrained family member would not be capable of the work. The prescribed difficult therapies are challenging to apply; taking a severe Traumatic Brain Injury patient successfully down the road is not an easy job for even a medical professional. Each injury is unique and demands customized therapies. When your brain circuitry is malfunctioning, your whole system is disarmed. Do not get disgusted if you think your loved one is not and will not try. Remember your loved one has a brain injury. Believe me, no one is more disoriented and confused than your loved one with a brain injury, and no one desires to recover more than he or she does.

I wrote about my remembered, unedited first days of awakening on auto pilot; the Enlightenment Section was written in its entirety in one sitting. I was in the state of Washington visiting a friend, Sue Sultze. At a horse show, an equine journalist, Kathy Bergh Peth, asked for an interview. Her interview opened doors that I had dared not; I let my twisted and tormented memories return to me when answering Kathy's pointed questions. I got up that night and wrote uncontrollably. That seems to be an established troubling pattern for me; once I start, it is hard to turn off my mind and let anything go. It was a cleansing relief to let the words and emotions gush out onto paper.

The first days of awakening show torment and

confusion. Don't be shocked or concerned if your loved one uses foul words; they are short, concise, and easy words to recall. This may happen even if profanity was not included in your loved one's speech patterns prior to the injury. Brain injury victims and stroke individuals often experience frustration and anger; possibly it comes out in the form of four letter words. Please give them grace, and wait to admonish or to hush them; any voice is a good voice. I found regaining ability was precious and empowering; even a poor improvement is a gain.

I fought to overcome the physical and mental unacceptable actions. I wanted power, and this desire led me to do some minor self mutilation. One torturous episode was enough; the medical staff could tie me down and attempt to restrict me, but no one could control or stop me, entirely. I had held onto some negative powers; I was able to damage myself while tied in bed. Although, by morning, I recognized that it was the "Crazies" winning and I must never ever hurt myself again.

Throughout the telling of my recovery story, I am sharing the story from my heart, sharing from my altered personality with troublesome quirks, disorders, and a skewed unique thought process. Blessed, I now have peace within myself.

At the Elk's Rehab Facility, I was operating while maintaining an "out of body experience." It was as if I was separated from myself and I was an observing spectator to my own daily functions; I hovered in the room in an empty space above the action. While talking to others who have survived a TBI, I have found this "out of body experience" is not an uncommon phenomenon amongst severe Traumatic Brain Injury sufferers.

No sane, healthy, sober person could imagine the feeling of dire solitude that surrounded me; I had abandoned myself. I had misplaced God and my faith due to the injury; I was ashamed and hiding. My brain data was mostly erased and I was all alone and hopeless.

My clear memories began only after my mom left me and the rehabilitation facility. As long as Mom was with me, I felt safe; I did not need to be in survival mode. Mom was saving me. She saw to my every need. I could trust her to keep me safe. Then Mom left, and I found that I was alone. I had to help myself. I think this revelation shows an extremely hard truth: if you want your loved one to use all of his or her will and strength to rise up and recover, the caregiver, spouse, or parent must step away and put the decisions in the hands of a top notch rehabilitation center and allow the therapists to do their jobs. I believe, if my mom had stayed, I never would have gotten low enough or scared enough to have had my survival mode kick in and go to work. I am not saying abandon your loved one; rather, force your loved one to be partially responsible, and let human nature do the rest. The will to live is huge in the survival process. You can check in by phone every day and visit in the evenings, but stay out of the rehabilitation process until your loved one reaches a successful point in their recovery to be sent home for you to continue the good work.

Few high-level traumatic brain injury victims recover enough to be cognizant, tell their memories, and share their struggles. I wrote this next section, ENLIGHTMENT, verbatim and without embellishment. It came rushing back through my memory when I chose to allow my mind the painful recall. Hopefully, my recitation will give you clarity into what your loved one may be struggling to overcome, or some other version equally troubling. There is no planned lesson book or map on the recovery of a TBI to prepare the caregivers. Comprehension into your loved one's changed life and mind as he or she is now living and thinking is an important thing for the caregiver to delve into and work to understand. The caregiver needs to adjust and apply your efforts to help your loved one return.

# Enlightenment

**Patient:** Robin M. Ross - Brain Injury Survivor
**Place:** Idaho Elks Rehab Brain Injury Unit
**Date:** June 1994

I struggled to resurface, but something was very wrong. My brain felt heavy and full of mud. The surgery site in my skull ached with intense pain where the bone flap had been removed and then replaced. I had no memory of surgery; I just knew I hurt. What's the deal? Where was I? Who was I? I did not recognize the room and could not focus my sight, and there was two of everything. Why a strap across my lower torso in a hospital bed with high sidebars up? Help! Let me go! Am I a prisoner and why?

My nurturing mother has made her exit. She is hoping to force me to climb another hurdle, to cope, and to awaken fully. Prior to this, I was in a limbo state, knowing she would see to my every need. Now, where was she? What is she thinking? Who is going to brush my teeth? I need Mom! About this time of panic, Dee Dee Bruneel came into Room 10B. She was an extremely caring, compassionate certified nurse's aide. Mom had asked her to keep an empathy filled eye upon me. Once again, I have a positive force carrying me on. I transferred my affections to Dee Dee with the absence of my mother.

"Please! Oh, please!! Someone come and get me! I NEED to go home! I can become and make Robin reappear. If only normalcy would occur. My head must quit screaming, and the hurting must stop!" Robin came back. I feel her hiding in the room. Robin is hiding and observing from a vantage point up high in the corner!

Dee Dee takes a moment to stop in my cell and say hello. Thank God! Here is someone I think I know and I like; she sees that I am here and I am sure she does like me. She loosens my waist binder, which gives me both mental and physical release. I wish Robin would come home to join me. Ooh! I am tired, and my skull aches through and through. Dee Dee lingers a while; this kind eyed lady's presence gives me peace of mind and a feeling of safety. Whew, I think I will get back in my warm mental cocoon and rest a while. The mud is thick and sticky in my head.

I don't have freedom of movement within the unit. An aide came and wheeled my chair and me to supper. Who is this bald, pathetic individual riding peaceably in a wheelchair? Cripples and sick people act like this. I won't!! I am not!!

Oops! Maybe, I was a bit premature; riding securely in a wheelchair is good, and I am showered sitting in one. Showering in the chair is preferable to the steel bed I laid upon for my first few showers. I am fed sitting in a wheelchair. Dee Dee rescues me by working harder. She appears every morning by 6:00 a.m. and rousts me out. She uses a rough kind of manner that I understand. In a few days, Dee Dee helps me learn to use a walker. A therapist had set me up and started us going with it in physical therapy. A temporary thing Dee Dee assures me. Even a walker, I soon will not need. Dee Dee is not condescending; she merely demands improvement and expects it, and I struggle to give it.

My mom has put out the effort to brief everyone involved in my healing process. She told them of my prior personality. She shared my character strengths and my weaknesses—show-off, brash, overachieving, positive, strong, willful, and competitive. Dee Dee puts these factors to work for me; she reaches down into my dark mental haze. I want to show her Robin can and will be back with all of her strengths and abilities!

Some of the nurses see me as a job. They see a partial, less-than-perfect person. I do not like them. I feel their smugness with a possibly imagined sense of self-superiority. They never touch me; they only put my meds in a cup and set it in my palm, and issue a command to "swallow." A smile and concern with a light touch would have made the medicine more welcome.

The nursing staff has a daily morning wakeup ritual of "What day is today?" "Who is the president?" "How are we today?" I HAVE HAD IT! "Don't talk down to me!" I scream from within. Instead, I answer her "How are we today?" inquiry with, "Well, I am a head injury, and you are an overweight, repetitive bore. Whew!!! Out of the room she waddles. She must have had herself excused from being one of my caregivers; I do not recall ever seeing her again. At times, my voice and my large vocabulary returns.

Then later my word recall falls apart. My hurt brain seems to stutter and stammer, and occasionally it stalls out.

It is after 6:00a.m., and I am back in my cell after my brain engaging and cooling daily shower. Dee Dee escorts (not wheels) me to the shower. The pulsating water beating down on my poor, naked, broken head feels so fine. It does help the pain and the lack of clarity. The water seems to clear the mud and reroute some circuits in my heavy head. Showering is one of my favorites, and brushing my teeth as well.

I am getting intense mental therapy now. The therapists are happy and enthusiastic. These people all know my name—I am not just a "B. I."(Brain Injury) to them. I am Robin. I am special! Somewhere hidden deep inside of my smashed brain is me! Robin is coming back. Watch out! Do not mess with me. Just show me the way, and move over.

Uh oh, more confusion! Can I do this? Embarrassed, Robin does not hang around. It is so hard. What is up with my emotions? Why are they torturing me? Where is Robin to the rescue? Help!!! I am only partly here, and my mind is broken. Dee Dee does not give up hope—she knows that Robin is coming back. Maybe she is right? She continues to challenge me to prove how special I am.

They took my walker away from me. I was swinging it around and clearing a path. Now, I have advanced to a cane with an accompanying bellyband for safety. I am able to perambulate down the hall and around the corner to the cafeteria. I sit at a table with older women; we have appointed seats. The morning conversation usually revolves around my companion's bowel movements—not an appetizing topic. The staff is proud of me. I clear my plate of all food. They worry about my swallowing, but no problem. I am not a baby! Dee Dee walks by my assigned seat with a smile and a touch. "Yes!" her look says, "We know Robin is here even more today than yesterday."

In my correct opinion, all the medical and health workers, families, and the support groups of the hurt or weakened person should realize this fact: The patient sees himself or herself reflected in a loved one's or a respected caregiver's eyes and believes the vision as the truth. Keep this in mind. Remember the power that YOU have to help your loved one overcome issues and return. Be sure not to add to your loved one's grief by showing negative judgment.

They have boosted my physical as well as mental therapy. I am so tired. Nearly every night, I go to my cell and my bed with ice on my head, and I am exhausted. Someone keeps my medicines straight. Someone keeps me safe. It is not my job. I am not my responsibility. Robin is still AWOL, but I do kind of like it here. I could not live on the outside. Real people scare me. I am sure they would know that I am off and that I am different. Anyone should be able to sense a weakness and a failing in me. I bet I emit an odor of fear.

I sit in the hall. I am afraid to be alone with myself. Robin will not stay with me. She is repulsed by my frustrated confusion and my pathetic physical shape. I am grasping and so lonely for human contact. Robin is sickened by my weaknesses and fears.

The Elk's allowed my brother, Bill, to take me from the Rehab. Bill, being my older brother, always had the job of being my champion. My niece, Sabrina came also. They drove me home for a day. I hated the frightening, hectic traffic. I am so fearful of anything hurting or touching my sad head. I am so TIRED! Stay back from me. Give me space! Many people came by our house to view me and judge my disabilities. Everyone stop looking at me! My muddy bald head throbs, and lights flash behind my eyes. Put me back in my safe cell. Where are my meds? I am glad to see my folks and my home place. "NO! Please take me back to the cloistered, quiet, safe medical facility, and hurry!" My dogs do not know me, nor will they come to me. How can this be? Oh yes, the real Robin is gone. I forgot for a bit, but my dogs know something is scary about me. Robin is missing, and their doggie world has totally gone awry.

I am glad the home visit was over. It was exhausting, and home is not yet for me. Sadly, I feel more at peace at the Rehab and definitely safer. I say over and over that I want to go home, but I am lying. Yes, I feel that I am a star at the Elk's Rehab Facility ; I am one among many damaged souls who can still shine once in a while. I belong here. I want to stay here. The public arena scares and it shames me! The therapists, mental and physical, are pushing me to my limits. I will show them who is strong and who is smart. Robin is on the edge watching—maybe, she will come back. I just wish the mud would clear and the weight would lift.

One day, I escaped the rehab facility; it was a step back to a short time of me being on 'Lock Down.' I stood and watched an employee punch in the exit code to a side door and leave; quickly by repeating over and over in my head the needed code, I entered it and slyly escaped. I rolled under a hedge next to the cool brick building wall; I stayed hid while they called and they called out for me. It was fun; I had power, again. After a bit of turmoil, I was found and taken back in the facility, I received no punishment beyond protecting me from myself.

My friends come often. Many times, I awake to find a familiar face setting at the end of my bed. Dianne brings me lunch, and she escorts me to eat outside on the grass. I can walk around inside now without an Elk's escort, with only a cane and sometimes with no bellyband. I have earned my freedom, and it makes me proud. Nancy and Jennifer, friends and good customers, hauled Gem Smoke, a horse I know and I trained along with their border collie, to the Elk's for me to touch and recall. The animals feel so right even with me standing on the asphalt in the city. My sense of smell is gone, but horse, dog, and outside odors are deeply ingrained and falsely recalled. I have flashes of Robin's life to which I must return. My friends keep seeking Robin to come out to meet the future.

Mom and Dad call me nightly. I receive so many phone calls that it irritates the facility and ties up their lines. Skip Brown, a successful California horse breeder/trainer calls; he is waiting for me, I will be fine—Robin will return, and we will have fun and success once again showing horses. Skip calls me nearly every evening; he calls my parents daily to provide support and understanding. Skip and Margie's son, Rusty, had a similar injury. Skip has already been down this road of working with a recovering head injury survivor. He has inside understanding of surviving a severe TBI; my family needed his positive thoughts and his offering of hope to lighten our load. Skip was my horse training mentor prior to the injury; I took him at his word and he had the power to stimulate me to try and succeed.

I am tired. I am always tired. I need more sleep. My head is full of mud and much heaviness. The Rehab's intelligence tests and mental responses are hard, but I can do it. I see Dee Dee daily, and she spurs me on. She assures me I am a winner.

The physical therapy is more and more. I hate being put on the little balance and exercise trampoline. I feel like a performing monkey. The spotters, standing around the trampoline, make me feel awkward and stupid. But, they are right—I may fall; I have fallen before.

I love to swim. I can find my balance in the pool. The water gives me buoyancy, and it cools my tired, aching head.

The therapists walk me outside, and we might even stroll on unleveled terrain. Often, they simply grasp the top of my waistband and lift—I very much resent the wedgies. Sometimes, they have me wear the bellyband and hold it. If they EVER remove this leash, I will be so pleased. Robin even visits for a while, although she is not her normal, pushy self. She is shy and concerned. Will Robin return full time? Wish I could see clearly. Wish I could think clearly. Wish my mud-filled head did not hurt.

Bill, my brother, comes to visit one day and takes me outside. We are all afraid I will topple. My pace is faltering and slow. The dead right leg betrays me—we keep the walk short. Yet, "outside" feels right and good, even though I'm city-bound and the space is filled with city noise.

The babies near the brain injury unit cry loudly at night. It breaks my heart. I will survive! I am not an innocent little victim. I do know never will I drink and drive or do any stupid selfish act to cause someone this type of devastation.

Next door is a young, quadriplegic mother of two little boys, Hillary. She named me "Butthead" and often calls out for my help. Yes, I am lucky; I can mend and I can help her too; I visit her often. She asks me to wipe her nose, which is scary because my hand eye coordination remains bad. Every time I whack her face or smash her nose we laugh. Laughter is good.

I maybe want to go home? Dee Dee thinks I will succeed and become me again. I still walk dumb and robotic with my cane, and my mud filled head still hurts and functions slowly.

The anti-seizure medicine has caused me to gain excessive weight. Plus, everything about me moves so slowly. I eat at every opportunity. Oh well, we are the same here—inmates with problems and weaknesses. I am one of the stoutest, and I do have mobility so I shouldn't whine. I could be the best of inmates; maybe I will stay and be a star; it would be easy.

Mom and Dad made their nightly call—they think Robin is back. I am sly and will let them think it is so; it makes them happy. This insecure, fumbling lump of ugly flesh is NOT the real Robin. I wonder: will she ever return? One night tied in my bed, I pinched and tore my skin. Anywhere there was a blemish, I tore at it. Self-injury gave me power. I was in control of the pain. No one noticed the bruises or bloody spots. I tore under my clothing; I hid my wild imaginings. I won't do that, again. I am not crazy! The Elk's is a kind, easier and safer world than the real pulsing world. Plus, I am "special" here. I am doing my best to meet everyone's expectations. I have stopped hurting myself and will never admit it. Honestly, I am NOT crazy!

I am a star!!! It is getting so much easier. Everyone here knows me, and I imagine they realize and think I am smart. They treat me somewhat like a puppy. They are so pleased when I am good; I get prizes and attention. In my devious, troubled mind, I know it does not take much to make me look good in comparison to some of the more injured; when allowed, I work the people and the system.

Dee Dee takes me back to the young quad's room often now. This girl will never be a star. I am afraid Hillary is all broken; I am fine, and I am stout. Robin will be back to save me from this degrading humiliation. Is the real world still there or is this my real world now? Dee Dee always asks for more effort; I fear she sees something the others do not. She is my anchor in these insane and turbulent waters. My head is still muddy, and I cannot make it clear. What is happening? Where did Robin go? The core and strength of her has left. Will she be back? Why did Robin have to go? Is it worth her necessary efforts to come back? What if Robin has made her escape and found it preferable to this Hell? SHE WILL COME BACK. . . ! She will??? Won't she?

In the evenings, my phone often rings; everyone wants Robin back. My family, old school mates, horse competitors, and a surprising number of normal people expect me to fully heal. They await my return back to the real world as my whole self and nothing less. People do not forget me; I wonder why? They must think I am special. What a good feeling to be special. Yes, I will quit faking and begin trying harder, as they may be right. Guess I will have to see. I want to be all I can be and more; each and every act of friendship encourages Robin to return.

Never doubt the strength of a loving gesture. We all need reassurance increased over and over if we have become "less" in our own self-appraisal. I worry that I am a little crazy; I know I am a lot scared. The inmates are here to be rehabilitated; we are definitely broken and need to be fixed. I hope that I can rejoin Robin before she gives up and flies away forever. It is awfully hard; the more I honestly strive, the more the therapists and the psychiatrists and the doctors ask of me. I am sure that they are surprised how well I am doing, and they have not seen anything.

I am having problems with my right leg being numb and my right arm atrophying—my arm is posturing. My center of balance is gone. I am anosmic; maybe it is a good thing not to be able to smell the odor of sickness; it does not compute and repulse me. Whenever I relax, my body curls, and I begin to rock back and forth. Again, I realize this is not acceptable. I am so tired. When will it end? Am I insane? Once again, many of the nurses refer to me as "Brain Injury" and not Robin. What do they know? Should I be ashamed? When will normalcy reoccur? And what will happen for Robin and me?

I have gained total freedom of movement within the facility now. My trusty cane and I can travel. I receive few hated wedgies! I am threatened by the motorized wheelchairs; they might run me down as they zoom down the halls and around the corners. NOTHING can be allowed near or threaten my head. Prior to the injury, there was a small bubble around my body that others should not invade. Now the bubble is much larger. Please, respect my space! Wow! Where is Robin? She is big and tough on her feet.

I need her solid strength to see me through; Robin and I can conquer and accomplish anything! But, do not get near my head!

Dee Dee is walking me further down the hall to a more private and grownup shower. I like it; I am proud of myself. The cool water feels so good on my poor, broken, fuzz-covered head. I bet Robin is watching me and must want to come back.

I am starting to feel a bit superior. The woman I see reflected back from Dee Dee's eyes is a bit lacking and deceitful. Once again, Dee Dee makes me see reality. I must dig deeper to find and rescue the real whole Robin before she smothers. Dee Dee keeps me honest.

The vocational therapist suggests that I change careers. Then why struggle to get well? What is this therapist thinking? The partnership with my parents, my work, the horses, the people, and the will to compete and to be a champion are my identity. Robin will NEVER come back if I don't return to the top of my game. I will just have to whip up and find myself. I really would like to rest; please for a time, just let me rest. Maybe, I can go home, and Robin will be there. Jesse, my Rottweiler, will know me this time; I will be the complete me.

They have me working hard. My hair is now prickly and fuzzy. It is like the Sampson and Delilah story. I lost my strength when they shaved off all of my long, red hair. I wear an eye patch, which I transfer from eye to eye trying to strengthen each of them and get the optic nerves to reunite. I look like an unattractive pirate with this getup. I still have double vision, which makes my stomach sick. I am getting fat and out of shape.

I am having horrid dreams of blood and gore. What is triggering these terrifying and mutilating dreams? My head spins and it hurts, and it is filled with white lights and gruesome explosions. I wake up sweating and fearful that these thoughts are real and not nightmares coming from something trapped within. Is it Robin? I won't even think about it now. I just wish the bad dreams would stop and give me peace.

I miss both my mom and Robin. I am having flashbacks of Mom being here. I still don't know why she abandoned me. She kept me safe, and she loves me. She softly rubbed my mud filled, cracked head by the hour!

I remember Mom and I went to St. Luke's Hospital in a rehab van for more tests. Some laughing kids pointed at me. I remember barking and growling while wheelchair bound at the dirty little snots. The cowards screamed and fled. I bet I left an impression they will not soon forget. I wonder how they will survive life and all of its possible pain and disappointments?

Often now, I find myself rocking back and forth. I have some kind of out of control cadence counting within my head. *0, 1, 2, 3, 4, 5, 6, 7, 8, 9, 10, 11, 12, 13, 14, 15, 16, 17, 18, 19, 20, 21 big breathe 21, 20, 19, 18, 17, 16, 15, 14, 13, 12, 11, 10, 9, 8, 7, 6, 5, 4, 3, 2, 1, 0!* Then ready, set, go! I am released and can springboard onward down the road of life. I do this repetitively throughout my day—it is so exhausting and upsetting. Robin must be horrified. Some degree of craziness and retardation has set it. My right arm and wrist is trying to drop and atrophy more all of the time. I still see double. I hear Robin screaming, "Try harder you brain injured weakling! Get control!" I am frightened; I can tell even Robin is scared.

Thank God! Dee Dee drops by with an encouraging word. Robin always appears for her. I doubt that Dee Dee realizes how important she has become. I listen for her footsteps in the hall and ache for her gentle, rewarding touch.

The phone rings, and it is Skip; later, Dad and Mom call. I receive many calls and letters. I am loved, and everyone, but me, knows this is only a temporary stage in my life. They must be right; they are no nonsense kind of people. I trust their judgment. When will my parents come with Robin and rescue me? I am nearly ready to rejoin normal people. I count my "21 cadence" and imagine myself fleeing home and then count "21 to 0" and finally relax. It is going to be fine with time. Everyone says "Patience." Patience, how can they imagine? Some people say, "I know how you feel." They do not—they don't have a clue, and I hope they never know. They are just ignorant.

I recall all who remembered and strengthened me—they kept Robin coming back. These people will remain treasured throughout my lifetime. They joined me in my lengthy battle to return. I am blessed; my friends and family are amazing and strong. They helped me to remain in the game. I will be a formidable player, again soon!

I wish the babies would stop crying. There is pain and frustration all around. Really, things do not look too bleak for me. I am a winner, and I will survive.

My step is still not firm. I used to be as solid as a brick outhouse. Now, I feel like a malfunctioning robot. If only I saw one clear image instead of a distorted double-view. I keep having and tasting blood soaked dreams. I never see me in the dreams.

It is night; I am alone. The Elk's staff is less. Someone sets me near the window and ties me upright in a comfortable enough position; I do not like it. But, like a vacant zombie, I stay. I am not capable of moving myself. The Boise River Festival Fireworks is happening tonight, and no one explained to me the noisy firework loaded event. I am confused! So confused and so very tired. The bright lights and exploding colors make my stomach sick and my head so SCARED! Is this the 4th of July? I hear loud, unpleasant laughter in the hallway. I resent this. What can be so funny? I see nothing to laugh about.

I do laugh during the day when Dee Dee is here. She makes me laugh often and long. One of her best kept secrets is knowing that laughter and smiles are riches much greater than gold. Neither anger nor pity, self pity included, has any place in the healing process. I am so tired of being watched, poked, prodded, and pushed. I just want and need to rest and become "Me," again. My head will not direct me to perform normally and with ease. Will I ever see "normal Robin" in the mirror, again?

Six a.m. "Get your lazy butt out of bed!" It is Dee Dee! I would do almost any tough task for her smile and her approval. I struggle from my bed and pick out the day's clothes. I am ready to make the odyssey to the shower stall waaaaaay down the hall. Dee Dee barely waits. She knows I can and I do keep up to her step with my cane clonking along.

Some of the wires between the computer in my head and the functioning powers in my body seem to have been severed. But, for Dee Dee's approval, stout Robin would return and splice them back into service. It seems remarkable how the right approach to reach my character and personality quirks succeeded. Dee Dee put out the extra effort to evaluate me and work me; with love and common sense, she did tunnel through the murky, muddy haze and grasp my soul to make me try.

How incredible is God's plan—that Dee Dee and I could live our lives at the same time on this Earth and come together in friendship.

I have lots of company. Many people from the outside filter in to help me see the light of day. Robin wants to come out and play; I fear I may never be complete. Venturing out is a scary event, but to think of staying hidden ranks with impossible. It is like Robin is caught in a spider's web. The web stretches and gives, but won't quite let us pull to freedom reunited as one. The effort is exhausting. A mealtime routine of getting a loaded fork of food speared and into my hungry mouth takes an immense, concentrated effort. Life is hard and makes me tired.

Life used to be so easy and rewarding. I was invincible; now I am afraid. I wish I would have realized these things and enjoyed all of its goodness.

The staff keeps waiting for me to pee in my pants. It is odd that my bodily functions are everyone else's business. I have been told over and over that B.I.'s are incontinent and once a brain injury always a brain injury. I will prove them wrong; Robin would never soil or urinate on herself.

I am afraid now. There is a possibility. . . I am insane. I am excellent at role playing. When visitors come, Robin appears for a time. She gives this pathetic and crippled puke a fine sense of humor and the necessary strength to please my company. When they leave, Robin flees the scene, leaving my head so tired and heavy after the performance. I am a sly, devious soul. If I do well enough, I will make my escape home and maybe coax Robin into revisiting this shell and live here within me. If I close enough doors in my head, Robin will have to come out of the maze and return to stay.

I do not feel the senseless need to act for Mom nor Dee Dee. They realize that this poor, trapped bug has about succumbed and will remain entangled forever in the sticky web, unless we honestly work to pull me free. They love the real me, not the image that I try to portray. The elastic cable of the web stretches and keeps me dangling. I have lots of help cheering me on. Other people give me their combined strength. I must endure and manage to break free. Robin has to reappear and pack this shadow up and out of here and head on home.

The Elk's Rehabilitation Facility has put me through a broad spectrum of tests. They gave me psych tests, cognitive skill tests, cooking tests, and hygiene tests. They tested me on my necessary daily skills. Before they would release me, I had to prove myself. We had a family Elk's Staff meeting. They decided that we all had passed. The jury was in—I could go home at the end of the week!!! Robin was here all day and for most of the harrowing tests. She pleased them. They set us free!

I know my parents can unite Robin within me, again. They will help and make me sort my thoughts. As a family, we can do anything. Besides, I have to get back to work. I have horses to ride. We are working people, so let's get to it! 0, 1, 2, 3, 4, 5, 6, 7, 8, 9, 10, 11, 12, 13, 14, 15, 16, 17, 18, 19, 20, 21—21, 20, 19, 18, 17, 16, 15, 14, 13, 12, 11, 10, 9, 8, 7, 6, 5, 4, 3, 2, 1, 0—*sigh*! Please, let this craziness end. I am SO tired. The horrid, bloody nightmares return. I won't tell anyone about these. It is another secret to be shared only with Robin; she will keep quiet.

The therapists cooked a "goodbye barbeque." I will miss most of them. The Idaho Elk's Rehabilitation Center is a great and much needed facility.

Dee Dee gave me a beautiful, hand-beaded buckle from her Native American heritage. She signed the card, "Friends Forever." I do not consider Dee Dee only a friend. She is blood and a part of me, for she has seen within, and she still cares for me. This bond proves good things can arise out of bad. She met me at my very lowest and pulled me out on the briny, drowning depths of despair. I love her.

Robin checks in more regularly now. I see and feel glimpses of her, often. She is like a deer in the headlights. She and I will make a positive high leap and outrun the danger. People will be surprised when I return; I will be stronger than before. A healed and scarred soul is tougher than an unblemished, unchallenged, and unproven one.

I am going home tomorrow. Mom was taught how and when to give me the anti-seizure meds, the mood altering meds, and all of the others. She will keep me safe. I wish someone could stop the nightmares. Maybe, I will not need the whole Robin to survive. At the earlier evaluation meeting, Dad and the original confident Robin proved they were willing and able to help mold me back. Dee Dee packed my clothes and my belongings. The leave taking is sad, and another unknown hard adventure begins. Now, I can see a light at the end of the tunnel. The bright light is HOME and NORMALCY shining. I do clearly see the entire healed Robin in the distance.

*End of Enlightment Section*

## My Experiences and Next Steps

Many people with head injuries have a resulting change in their personalities. I became aware of possible life threatening injury, and fear entered my world. Agoraphobia had me in its grasp; this is an extreme anxiety disorder with crippling fear of leaving your safety area. I refused to leave our property unless with my Mom or two other close friends. I simply could not leave the shelter of our ranch. Prior, I had always felt that I was invincible and I was comfortable with myself.

Competition has stayed alive in my scattered

thoughts; this personal attribute serves me well. I was blessed with parents who shaped me to feel special and capable; I was taught to approach everyone with respect. I was taught to keep inquiring and following the greatest in the profession of your choice. Reach for the stars instead of the mediocre.

The top horse trainers in the nation are my friends and mentors. The best in our industry is whom I approach. People like to help an admiring and improving person; the ego is a powerful motivator. To quote Doug Williamson, a Million Dollar National Reined Cow Horse earner, AQHA World Champion, Hall of Famer, and my good friend, "Winning isn't everything; it is the only thing."

I have been a winner; I rode a horse well and had good basic skills with athletic ability. With guidance and good horses, it was easy, fun, and rewarding to compete. I had a near photographic memory. The strong basics I had been taught about life, my family genetics, and my trust in the Lord and His grace, helped me conquer most past struggles.

With the resulting temporary disabilities from the devastating injury, slowly came a better sense of understanding and gratitude. I am a kinder more empathetic person. I recognize limitations are not necessarily a sign of weakness or lack of heart.

People supposedly are created equal. Equal opportunity is not equally distributed due to physical differences, financial standing, and many other attributes. You have to play the hand of cards that you are dealt. Don't be angry. Instead, be decisive. Change what is changeable, and make life the best it can be. When a door closes in your life choose to make this opportunity into a new positive start; choose a new beginning and move faithfully onward.

Consider that your loved one may be tortured by confusion and may have lost his or her sense of reality. Possibly, your loved one is not feeling sane and does not recognize who he or she is; keep this valid concern in your mind and in your heart. Work towards improvement, but remain realistic and methodically positive.

At the Rehab, I was toileted many times a day. The medical staff was positive that I would be incontinent. They watched me for seizures. They kept stating that seizures were a huge possibility in my future. Remember your loved one may be listening and believing, especially if hearing respected medical personnel stating an opinion. Showing and expressing the constant worry of my probable incontinence showed up to haunt me when my memories returned at a later date.

Every morning at the Rehab, my table companions spoke happily and with great description of their bowel movement. Any physical accomplishment had taken a huge importance in their daily ritual, and these women were obsessed about it. Regaining control of any issue is worth telling and sharing. They were proud of accomplishment and normal bodily function. It's hard to understand this concept, as bowel movements are not the best topic for breakfast conversation. Healthy people take body function for granted and don't spend time considering the effort our brain puts out every minute of every day to keep us alive.

While at the Elk's Rehab, I decided I was a grown woman and wanted to look like it. I could manage to put on my makeup and wear perfume. I was very aromatic and overly made up. I was content with my new look and was quite pleased to have accomplished it—always in my mind, it remained strong that I was not a baby. At the time, my choices were garish, but I soon evolved, and my appearance became acceptable. Remember not to discourage your loved one's growth even if it isn't totally acceptable. By letting your loved one come out of hiding and express opinions and personality, you are allowing him or her to rejoin society and be individually proud.

Highly educated people interviewed and studied me. The Idaho Neurological Institute gave me a complicated questionnaire. I was given a long, exhausting IQ test, twice. The Institute made their own deductions. They told me what I thought and what I needed; few listened to my full input. Listening is so important, and I feel the medical field could learn from my factual report and put it into successful application.

Study and know the pre-injury personality characteristics. Be aware of your person's history and lifestyle. Examine his or her existing personality. Create your own ideas, experiments, and avenues to reach and encourage your loved one.

The support group has to dig deeper into the meeker person's psyche. Give your loved one a reason to try. Recovery is hard work. Find the tougher part of your loved one. We cannot change who we were, but we can attempt to alter the new person. Not all of us are made of stern stuff; some people may need a softer nudge. The caregivers mold and shape the injured psyche. Engage your loved one in all the processes. Being included will make a huge difference to your loved one's efforts.

I never found the recipe to reach through the damaged brain and pull out the original person. You may never see the original person again. You, as a caregiver, must help to figure out your loved one's own path; always recognize it is not your path, but theirs.

We all can lose track of "normal." Age and time might diminish us. What is normal? I am referring to whatever would have been normal for this individual. Don't allow the injury to be a safe haven in which to hide from your responsibilities and self. I played the TBI card, and I over played it when allowed. As an excuse, I would say, "I am a head injury." Often, I was given a pass on my failures by surrounding people. Many do not have high expectations of head injured individuals. I was sly, and I knew how to take advantage.

Brutal honesty plays a role in recovery. One should concentrate on what the TBI can do and not waste time commiserating on what they can't. The injury happened; it is a fact. The next fact is that you need to strive to repair it. Don't stop working if you feel there is more your loved one can accomplish.

We all do only what life expects and demands of us. Help, but don't hinder by being kind. See what your person can do for him or herself. Accept the gesture when your loved one attempts to help, even if it causes you more work. I value myself by what I manage to get done successfully. Pride and ego motivates us to do better.

I have had no more seizures since the accident occurred. The day of the accident, I was found in the throes of a violent grand maul seizure. My head was bleeding profusely from the impact and crash to the hard ground. Remember, in the Rehab facility, I mentioned the staff worried that I might have a seizure at any time and spoke of it in my presence? That placed the idea solidly in my head, and I still am unduly concerned. What if out of fear, my parents had opted for me to stay on the mind altering anti seizure drugs? Tegretol filled my head with mud and was holding my thinking processes prisoner.

Don't talk in front of your loved one as if he or she is deaf and dumb; include them in conversations. Remember, your loved one may be hearing and retaining your future damning statements.

Years later, as I recalled my memories and the trauma, I did become incontinent. Not for long, but I think I lost control as the negative seed had been planted into my broken head by the power of repetition and suggestion. The Elk staff had put the thought and fear into my head; they had often verbalized their sureness that I would be incontinent. Months later, when I first opened my mind to remember my lost days, I started wetting my pants. I was mortified, but I was blessed, as I could reach out to Dr. Jutzy at his home. I asked him, "How long will this continue?" He said, "I don't know."

Then he said, "How long do YOU think it will last?" What a great way to put control back into my hands. He gave me power. It worked; I regained my dignity. The incontinence stopped.

I had a brain injury; I am not a Brain Injury. It is an accepted therapy protocol to anger brain injured people. Anger is a big emotion. Maybe anger does make you dig deeper, causing you to pull up and use this strong emotion. In my presence, they would say, "Once a brain injury, always a brain injury." Make me mad? That was too easy. I was angry and confused from the beginning. The stouter minded individual will work to prove that he or she can overcome the injury. The meeker person may need more help and persuasion. "Once a brain injury, always a brain injury" if told to a submissive individual by a doctor might become your loved one's truth and take over his or her weakened state of mind and identity. Your loved one may stop trying; remember, but for the grace of God go you.

One change that I would like to see become protocol to the medical staff and anyone that had daily contact with me was to learn my name and please use it. Some would say, "Get the brain injury" or "Bring the brain injury." Why did they not show some polite manners and learn my name? My name was on all my charts and written on the door of my room at the entry point. Once again, common sense and human kindness enters the arena.

I was starved for human touch. When they gave me my daily meds, it would have been nice to have had my hand touched. An encouraging squeeze of the shoulder would have meant a lot. Some of the nurses would set the Dixie paper cup in the open palm of my hand, supply the glass of tepid water, flatly say "take your meds," and sternly wait until I tossed and I swallowed.

In my case, I had a strong sense of spirituality and the Lord; which I did displace for a time. I now have a stronger one. God does not heal you just through prayers. He will answer; His answer may be "NO." The Lord works on his own schedule. We need faith, and we have to work and work some more to dig out of the muddled place in which we fell. The Devil is busy causing evil and hate. Never say to the brain injured person, "God must love you" or "God has a plan." What a huge amount of pressure you just put on that poor confused person. God doesn't love that person more or less—God loves everyone. People die. God does not kill them; God loves them. The happenstance of evil comes from the Devil and his demons or possibly from humans making poor choices.

Sometimes, I think, there is no reason, but evil. The Devil makes use of our poor or dangerous choices. Don't add guilt to your loved one's load for surviving. I did and do feel a strong guilt for living. Think before you speak. Kindness and common sense again.

After going home with my parents, I needed constant monitoring. My residence was on our family ranch. Mom moved in to my nearby home for a time. Dad came to my house for her tasty home cooked meals. Mom stayed with me for days; I needed her. I forgot to turn off water. I left the burners on the stove hot. I fell. I could not manage my seizure meds, mood elevators, or my pain pills. Plus, I was fearful of seizures and lapses in my own mind.

My intelligent mother put me on a daily schedule. My amount of food intake lessened, and the treats were reduced. She woke me early and got me started. I did need a lot of sleep. Narcolepsy had hold of me; I fell asleep and slept much of the day. Currently, I still sleep long and hard. I need excessive sleep to function well. In my case, a tired mind is a dysfunctional mind.

Mom fed me a balanced diet. She saw to my hygiene. She exercised me mentally. Mom knew my prior preference of reading material, and she researched the authors I had read. She obtained their books and placed me in my recliner to read. The double vision made it hard, so she found books with big type. I either wore the eye patch or kept one eye shut to stop the double vision problem. She made sure that I rotated the patch to strengthen both eyes. She started with easy books and then moved on to complicated mysteries and complex plots as I begin to have better reading skills and retention. Then she would question me and make me recall the prior day's reading. She gave me tests as to the character's names and their individual roles in the books. My mother, when she feels it is needed, can be a powerful little tyrant. She was sure that with both of our work and effort that I would be capable, again. My short term memory had no chance to stay hidden. Seldom, did I get away with playing the 'Poor Me, I am a Brain Injury' card.

Mom helped me do my exercises, and she kept count. First, we walked around inside my large home. Next, we barely got off the front step and walked outside on the deck. Then she made the large accomplishment of guiding me down the stairs. We went a few steps with me walking beside her, slowly and labored, while wearing the bellyband. The supporting leash was in her capable hand. She upped my walking distance daily and my speed. "Just a few more steps," she would say. It was always, "Just a few more steps." Soon, we were walking over the bridge to the barn, next down the dirt lane to the mailbox. More was always better. Speed and better cadence of gait came. Learning to run took much more coordination than I could put together for years. I still run disjointed. Today, riding a bike remains disastrous.

Bicycling was a strong muscle memory as a kid. Now, I can pedal, but stopping usually entails a tip over. No big deal; I enjoy walking. Within my family, whining is not allowed. If you don't like it, then fix it. Search hard to find another way. I walk every day to stay fit and to clear my mind. Walking eases stress and discourages depression.

Luka, Jed and I have walked the stresss and worries from my mind many times. Dogs rock!!!

I find myself improving and changing daily. I was and I remain extremely competitive. Not all people operate on that system of being the best in every situation; so, let your loved ones live their lives accordingly. Don't give up your own life nor ignore your remaining family, as they need your attention and love too. Perfection is the goal, but improvement is the realistic true hope.

I was very FEARFUL, and life is scary at times. People wanted to take me out and do things like go to a movie. The last thing I wanted to do was be seen and judged or get out of my safe zone. Consider that with your person. I was overwhelmed and frightened by changes. I was on the outside of life looking in. Don't bully your person. Reconsider the kind, common sense elements, and make your decisions wisely. Believe that sometimes your loved one might know best. Being a caregiver is a balance of yes's and no's with a balance of applause versus admonishment. Stay real, and stay in the game to win if possible.

Huckleberry is my service dog. His strength and love give me responsibility and self-confidence. I worry about him instead of myself. I no longer fear and fight the crowds; he keeps me feeling safe. I know Huck loves me above all things.

Seek professional help. Never be too proud or foolish to search out therapists for physical and mental guidance. Let the injured person talk it out to a good listener. Then plan on listening some more. The grief I felt was like the death of someone I loved and I needed. In my head, it was the death of me. I was compelled to talk through it until I found myself, and talk I did and I continue to do so. Shared conversations have been a large part of my healing process.

There are definitely stages in which I traveled. I was confused, then angry, then confused longer, then embarrassed; I was obsessive beyond belief. I counted over and over again. I was ruled by repetitive and compulsive acts.

There is a certain stigma to being a brain injury. I felt it meant less than being smart. This made me angry and confused again. What could be done to save me? I was so confused and my head so heavy and full. I was blessed, as I had someone to lead me home and onward. I traveled through depression, shame, resignation, surges of strength to overcome, then times of weakness and sorrow, I stuttered, I cried, and I could not think of words. My inherent personal hardiness (plain ole stubbornness) played a strong roll. I know often God was carrying me; He never left me.

It was a long, harrowing road; I made the journey back to wellness, possibly so can your loved one.

Remember, your intelligent, caring help could be making an amazing difference and possibly be directing your loved one's destiny.

After the injury, I gained a lot of weight prior to Mom having control of my food intake. The extra weight made my every movement harder. This lack of mobility and the fact that I was an excellent eater helped to put on the pounds. Many TBI's have poor appetites; your brain and body must be fed to heal. I knew this from caring for sick or injured animals; a competent horse owner stalls the sick or injured animal, adjusts their food intake and exercises with care.

At the Elk's Rehab, they gave me a menu for every meal every day. I diligently filled it out; I marked everything, and they delivered it to my table. If I had a clean plate at the meal's end, I received a star. I had many stars! For example, the breakfast menu offered hot cakes, Cream of Wheat, bananas, eggs, toast, cold cereal, milk, a sweet roll or two, bacon, and a slice of melon. Lacking judgment and with the failure of the staff to monitor me, I ordered and consumed it all. Common sense intervention to control my consumption would have been preferable to help me manage my weight. The kitchen dietician supplied the huge meals, and an aide fed me. It got worse after I could finally feed myself. I do remember the first time that I trapped a pea on a fork and gobbled it down; I was an eating machine. The nurses and therapists liked their crazy star collector. They brought me good Starbuck's coffee and also treats from the kitchen throughout the day. I never ever refused a sweet. My gluttony is a result of the brain injury and remains a mental battle.

I ate for control and to forget my pain and deficits. Shoving something into my mouth seems to calm and make me happy. My neurosurgeon explained that the near death injury brought PTSD along with the recovery. Now, I choose to think that I can overcome and not hide behind the injury. Being fat is not an option; I hate it, and it hurts my body. Conquer each day, and the results will be positive. Don't expect to improve by even 1% daily; in 100 days, your loved one would be 100% improved. Be realistic. There will be bad days as well as good days in every change you try to improve and put in place.

My normalcy differed after the accident. What and who would have I been if I had not lost the productive years of my life? I continue to strive to find a plateau of real and to be accountable in my changed world and with my changed self. There is no use looking back and asking "what or who." There is only now and the individual that you have become. This is an unalterable fact in everyone's life.

I have a learned understanding of the possibility to recover and the process involved. The brain injured person is not going to recover on his or her own; a severe Traumatic Brain Injury disables clear thinking. The job of the caregivers and support group is to provide the proper stimulus to help the individual strive to return. I repeat this important, proven thought over and over in my message. It is my desire to assist the families and surrounding people. Be prepared for some rough water as you guide the injured loved ones down the rapids.

I was fairly obtuse. People could not win. If I crippled into a room and no one gave me their chair, then I was mad. Couldn't they see that I was hurt? Yet, if someone quickly gave me their chair, I was mad. Did they think I was a cripple?

Allow some margin of error to the person you are helping. It is hard, and it is embarrassing to know that your brain is damaged and that you are not running on all cylinders. But, in the end, the brain-damaged person must take responsibility for his or her actions and speech. I worked the system, often rude, unless I met a stronger personality than my own. Then I would rein it in and act accordingly. Sometimes, you need to exhibit strength to encourage your loved one and make him or her respect you in the process.

The cane became an extension of my arm. The Elk's Rehab staff had to make me accept a reprimand or lose the cane. The cane was my mobility, but my aggressive actions became dangerous.

One day, I used my cane and poked a male nurse hard in the chest for what I considered mean and rude behavior; he was loudly bossing Dee Dee. In my mind, Dee Dee was above reproach; I was going to stop anyone abusing her in any way. Traumatic brain injuries often become overly protective of important people in their immediate circle. Now, I mostly have the anger and physical issues under control. It took a huge effort to understand that it is wrong to be combative. I have no special rights merely because I had a head injury with confused emotions; get over it.

One of the worst things for me was when I was told "No." This word made me feel like a less than intelligent child. I took personal insult from hearing "No." In fact, today, I still have trouble wrapping my mind around needing to alter my course and accept an unconditional "No."

A good caregiver gives sympathy, love, motivation, or acceptance with a "No" thrown in once in a while. The hurt person better learn to handle "No." Life has unexplained "No's" that must be dealt with. Most of the time, I knew right from wrong. Sometimes, I chose wrong in hopes of getting away with it. A caregiver has the hardest, most important job of all. Don't implode. Take some time for yourself, and do expect to have a meltdown occasionally.

Within the professional Cow Horse world, my success story is well known. We are a tight group of competitors. Many people and valued friends rallied around me in my time of distress. We received phone calls and cards from hundreds of people around the world and across this great nation. My childhood heroes are my proven friends.

I hope that my actions and my strong will imprints good behavior and success on others. While at the horse events, often I am approached concerning my medical history. My goal is to be a positive example of recovery. I got well, and I believe that nearly every person's life status after an injury can be improved. A winning attitude is an acquired element. Let us unite and help each and every person to become a winner and the best that they can be.

As you travel down this road attempting to guide your loved one, you are going to find potholes and meet detours or stop signs. Never hesitate to ask for help. Qualified people are out there and happy to assist.

We all love a success story. Do your best to map and to live your own success story. Be patient in its growth, but do not stop climbing toward wellness.

In my experience, the government aid and Social Security Insurance is not built to reward recovery. I think it should be merit based and provide encouragement, both financial and personal. I don't think they are looking for success stories. I was denied any assistance, as I refused to say that I was not getting better every day. I would not stay in my wheelchair, continue stuttering, and be at a loss for word recall. The investigator and the SSI Judge said that I could be a towel folder or possibly a security guard. Ridiculous, at the time my night vision was bad and my confidence to drive limited. The SSI board said that getting to work was not their problem. I would not declare myself disabled or a cripple. If I had said that I was lacking and disabled, disabled is where I would have remained. I received no government aid. If not for my support group and family, I may have ended up living in a box under a bridge. Homeless could have been my address.

My dad had a below the knee prosthesis. He lost his leg in 1962 due to Osteomyelitis, bone cancer; simultaneously he contracted Spinal Meningitis. I was five at the time, and through the years, I never heard him complain. He refused to be thought of as disabled. A short time after his amputation, Dad was back on a horse and managing the family business. Out of necessity, he was back riding a horse with only one leg before his prosthesis was built to fit. I remember a neighbor stopping to tell Mom, "Johnny fell off in a mud puddle. He needs you to catch his horse. He didn't seem to want any assistance, but I think he needs your help." Yes, I come from tough minded, tough bodied people. We are survivors.

Now, I realize that being disabled is not shameful. To accept being disabled and for you not to become an asset to your community is shameful only if you could overcome and you do willingly make the choice not to improve. Please do not embrace your failures or hold your disability close.

I was blessed. My parents were in a financial situation that they could care for me and my needs. I did lose the best working years of my life. My poor health spent and devoured much of my parent's retirement.

My injury needed a professional rehab facility. I required qualified therapists. Allow the people who are experts in this field to assist and lead you through the recovery; they are specialists and trained. A normal person may have the desire, but not the in-depth knowledge.

The injured person is going to want to return home. I pleaded as soon as I began communicating. I wanted to go home! Later, I was scared to leave the confines of the Rehab Facility; but, I did not voice my feelings of insecurity; I knew it was expected for me to want to leave so I lied. I would not have recovered at home; thankfully my parents were wise and chose to leave me in good hands. The trained therapists put me through complicated, intricate mental games, puzzles, and tests. Physically, they pushed me nearly beyond my limits. They made me try harder every day and work to the extreme every session more than I thought possible; I got better, and their program worked.

Prior to the injury, I was marketing horses overseas for large sums. I was winning in National competitions. Post injury, I was struggling to regain my mind and my physical ability. My customers were gone. They took their horses and went to capable, healthy trainers. After the injury, I received no wages. I had nothing to offer; I sold no horses.

We relocated to Oklahoma from the northwest. It was necessary for me to remove myself from the people that knew my situation. The stigma and label of Traumatic Brain Injury was haunting me. Many people spoke overly loud and in baby talk voices as if I had no cognitive skills.

My parents sold our successful business of many years, our homes, and left our family behind to encourage and continue my growth. Moving to a new area gave me a clean slate and let me reinvent and remake myself. We relocated 1,700 miles away from the past. I didn't feel the failure of the "Traumatic Brain Injury" in every step I gained down here in Oklahoma. To be able to market talented, high-dollar horses and to win big events, you have to have the reputation of a confident, capable winner. I was able to put up a strong façade for a time. I have since retired from the very demanding world of the Cow Horse industry. My right leg and right side is affected with numbness and lack of strength. I am no longer competitive in this event. I suggest you be smart and search out options in which your loved one can succeed and excel. Always remember to be thoughtful and considerate and not to kill the passion.

Be aware, your loved one may be feeling total incompetency and regret being alive. You cannot know what is going on in his or her broken mind. I held my loaded gun and wanted very much to be strong enough to do the deed of termination. I recall sitting on the end of my bed with my comforting Smith and Wesson 38 pistol in hand while still in Idaho, then again after the positive move to Oklahoma—same gun, same bed, only a different state. I never reached the level of complete despair. God and "Hope" is what kept me determined. Life is a blessing, and God is always with you. Do not maliciously remove the Hope from their futures.

I have chosen to retire from our proven horse business and the stressful rigors of competition. The beautiful Cross J Horse Ranch and our homes are sold. Our horse herd is gone to live and prosper in other hands; I did keep ReyGuns Rosealee. Horses are too deeply embedded in my mind and my existence for me to become horseless. We are relocating to Guthrie, Oklahoma; a new chapter in my life has been started.

My conviction and purpose in life is to offer hope through Jesus Christ and to share His good news of eternal salvation through giving my testimony for all to read. He is real and He is alive; I have His Peace and His unconditional love. Why not choose Jesus and believe? To receive His many blessings all we need is to have Faith. Remember, you can choose whatever passion to energize and motivate your person then apply the principles of Traumatic Brain Injury & A Cowgirl's Return to find guidance and proven suggestions to recovery. I chose God, but the option pathway is open to whatever your person clings to and believes.

Choose any passion and find their burning interests to help your loved one return. It is in your hands as a caregiver to put them to work both mentally and physically. The best way to encourage growth is to give them some reasonable power of decision making and help to set their own goals. They may now have some child like tendencies, but they remain adults; respect them.

In 2004, with the help of friends, I established a nonprofit titled "ReBirth" to address TBI issues. At that time, I was not mentally or physically able to manage the business. It takes money and much effort to be successful.

I chose to discontinue the nonprofit after I realized it was going to fail under my leadership.

Now, I am promising my time and my efforts, and I continue to give my heart to God. I have reached a higher degree of wellness, and my goal is to help others recover. We must deny the Devil and his demons. Now is the time to share our Christianity and our blessings and praise God through Jesus Christ. This promising door is available for us all to open or we can leave it closed; you choose.

## Lifestyle Incentive of Animals: Horses & Dogs

Just days after being discharged from the Elk's Rehab while still living in Idaho, I would struggle with my walker into the back bedroom of my home. Looking out of a big picture window was fulfilling and placed positive dreams into my head. I could see lots of horses and much activity. I struggled into the distant bedroom so I could watch and concentrate on our handsome two year old palomino stallion in his turnout pen. He played and moved graciously around, content and happy. This special horse, in my mind, was a glorious, handsome boy of which dreams and hopes are made. I would think to myself, giving voice to my desires, "I am going to return, and I am going to win on you someday; I know I will." We had purchased Gold Hickory Chex as a six month old prospect for me to later train, show, and promote in the big events. His bloodlines would make an excellent cross on our mares. He is the sire of three of our best broodmares. I nicknamed him "Canary." He was one of the four I hauled to the show the day of my accident. It was not him that fell or hurt me on that fateful day.

Two different accomplished horsemen offered to show the yellow horse for my family, free of charge. To have either of these talented, nationally-known men promoting our future breeding stallion would have been a wise business decision, although it would have broken my heart to have Canary taken from me. Dick Pieper of Marietta, Oklahoma—an AQHA World Champion, NRHA proven Champion, NRHA Judge, an NRHA Hall of Famer, NCHA Non Pro Champion, and top breeder—was offering to take my horse to train and win. Also prior mentioned, Skip Brown from Red Bluff, California, an accomplished NRCHA Judge, and a top West Coast competitor, plus NRCHA Hall of Fame member and Top Breeder—made the exceptional offer to my parents days after my Traumatic

Brain Injury occurred. My parents realized my dreams and my goals linked to this particular horse; they said "No" to both men. They, my parents, wisely used my love for this horse to encourage me to stagger onward with determination, grit, and much hope. I would not win the bigger money competitions. This chance and their confidence in me and the yellow horse did help me win to find myself and return. I won in the arena of life by regaining myself and my good life. My parents knew they were sacrificing this good horse's possible big time career; the idea, the training, and the riding of this special horse did drive my recovery onward. Dick and Skip still advise and help me; they are great men and my treasured friends. The world is full of good people.

I did accomplish the goal of proving Canary a winner. After the Oklahoma move, this little compact built stallion and I won the Palomino Horse Breeders Association Amateur Working Cow Horse World Championship held in Tulsa. I was thrilled and happy. I know the Breed Shows are not as competitive as the NRCHA, but what a step to be able to remember the pattern and perform the complicated maneuvers! I was thrilled to be a player in any arena. Dad was proudly on the sidelines watching Canary and I prevail. To be on a talented horse and to remember the pattern and beat the competition was a dream come true. I did it; I beat my own limitations. On this day, I was not a disabled Brain Injury. My recovery was very linked to the yellow horse. He kept me dreaming and struggling to gain the ability to compete again. I was terribly frightened, but never admitted it. To admit fear, I would have had to quit.

I lied to myself and I struggled onward; I lied to everyone. I hid my fear and was secretly ashamed of my limitations. My parents and my friends had no idea. I hated going to the competitions for a time, yet Canary and I continued to win. My identity is wrapped up deeply with my accomplishments on a horse and the skill involved. I had to prove that I was back. I needed to prove it to me as well as other people. Canary was my partner in the show pen. A few special horses seem to rise to the occasion and take care of their rider. The yellow horse, even while being a breeding stallion, packed me around like I was a little kid. He got more spirit and aggression as I healed and regained my ability.

Life is best when you are making good choices. I was blessed with good friends and good horses. I managed to make numerous, positive, life-altering choices. Later, one such choice was lending Gold Hickory Chex to Stefanie LeGrande, EdD, MSN, RN. Stef needed a good, solid horse to show, and he enjoyed the game. Stefanie and I will always remain great friends. She helps me in many decisions and believes in my goal of providing "Hope." Once more a good choice led to more good choices and more blessed results; Stefanie and I are sisters in Christ.

Finally, with his advancing years, I gave Canary to a fine young woman with a sweet little girl. Canary was getting older and needing more care. A beginner rider who was happy not doing the rigors of tough competition suited him at this stage of his life. My good friend, Shannon Slavens, was able to provide for him in stabled comfort. Carefully, Canary packed her daughter around for a time. Caitlinn loved him, and he loved her; she was his little girl. Every horse needs his reward of a loving little girl. Currently, Canary is packing Caitlinn's grandma and one of Caitlinn's young female cousins. Canary, was good to me and I returned his love. As an obsessive TBI, I could never have abandoned him and went on my way; my thoughts are often written in stone and near impossible for me to release. Canary had needs to be met; I gave him a solid future by trusting his care to a knowledgeable person and my wonderful friend, Shannon.

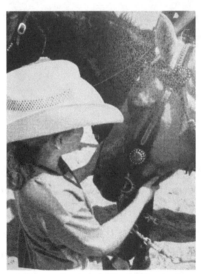

Canary earned & deserves a relaxed retirement,.
He loves his pampering.

Animals, especially dogs, supply unconditional love. They provide warmth. Caring for them brings a reward and a feeling of accomplishment, as you see to their daily needs. Work hard, but take the time to savor. Mostly, if you truly try, you can see goodness in near all things. Nature and animals are my grounding touch with reality.

They caused me to dig deep to return. What will help your TBI person struggle for recovery? God has provided many treasures for options. Use whatever reaches your loved one. It may not be God for your choice, but His is the path I chose, and look at me! Try asking God into your heart and receive his grace; what have you got to lose by asking?

Sadly, some of the Traumatic Brain Injured persons lived hard, empty lives before their injuries; these people may not have the strong desire to return. For them, I do not know any magical answers. If you are reading this, then you must care and are determined to help your loved one. That person is blessed to have you.

The more I worked, the more inventive the physical therapists became. A family friend and great PT, Jim Stiltz, worked with me after I returned home. Mom drove me to a nearby hospital twice a week to have Jim put me through my paces. One dramatic example was his inventive stairwell exercises. He would have me walk up the stairs and then he'd step back; I would step backwards facing forward while going down the stairs with him securely behind me at all times. I trusted Jim would not let me fall.

One day at the Holy Rosary Hospital in Oregon, during an extra challenging therapy session, I collapsed on the stationary bicycle. This intense overload may have helped my brain to create new neuron pathways. After an emergency call to my neurosurgeon, they laid me down and applied ice to my throbbing head. With most of the therapists, more was better. I still call Jim at his home, 22 years later, when I experience a pain or a weakness. He always takes the time to come up with an applicable exercise. This capable man would come to the ranch in Idaho after putting in his day's work at the Holy Rosary Hospital. He would drive extra miles to our ranch to explain a new idea and different therapy to Mom. No wonder, I got well. People are knowledgeable, generous, and kind. I say, "God is good."

I had a challenging, fun, hard life before my injury. To regain it was worth all the work. I am not completely back or totally capable, but I am comfortable being me; finally, I am at peace. Thankfully, I beat the medical prognosis. It did take over ten years for me to return to a competent level and my journey continues forward.

Before retiring from the demanding athletic events of the Reined Cow Horse, I gave it one last hurrah. Once again, I was blessed with a great horse. Some of the ole boys say, "One great horse is all you get." Not true; I had at least three great ones in my demanding career.

PG Rey Gun, a royally bred AQHA stallion and I won at the national level.

My goals were met; I had proven I was back. I could train a good horse and win, again. PG Rey Gun is an NRCHA Superior Reined Cow Horse shown only under my guidance.

My fears were continuing to get worse, and my limits more pronounced. I am no longer young; I kept getting hurt. I knew and feared it could be worse. I did make some great fence runs on this beautiful stallion, and I retired with pride. Currently, PG Rey Gun is siring winners and resides in the capable care and the ownership of Justin Reed Performance Horses in Mill Creek, Oklahoma. Horses, and horsemen, and women will remain solidly in my life.

My mounts often do win with other riders in the saddle. A good trainer makes and shows horses to win in tough competition. A successful, accomplished trainer strives for the wins. It is even better if their proven show horses continue to win for lesser riders and packs them around safely. God makes good horses. As trainers, we shape every horse's talents, but a good horse is good in spite of us, not because of us!

It is necessary to make goals, but do keep them realistic. Looking back, I was very foolish in my TBI post injury endeavors. I broke my leg twice, fractured a hand, broke ribs, tore my rotator cuff and had soft tissue injuries with more bruises and aches. What was I thinking?

Never, could I repeat this struggle and manage to return again. My head needed to be protected. The fact is if you are afraid of the water, you should stay out of the deepest area. I knew this reality, but determination pushed me onward. Doing the high-speed, wildly demanding fence work is definitely in the deep end of the competition pool. The last big cow horse event in which I showed, I had a separation of horse and rider. I hit my head on the fence wall; I was hurting and blood leaked from my left ear. It was at this time, I chose to retire from my beloved Fence Work competition.

NRCHA World Championships 2005, 11 years after the accident.

## Summary and Our Thoughts

The further time takes me away, the less the TBI causing accident seems real. I find myself wanting more; I forget to appreciate all regained. Remember to thank God often. Be joyful of the little things; appreciate and be thrilled by totally everything.

Be kind as your day moves onward. When you meet the eye of an injured person or a frail older person, offer a smile and a nod of respect, encouragement, and acceptance. I am not all sweetness and light, but my goal is to purposefully never act mean or hateful. It is rewarding and heart-lifting to do a good deed; in most instances you will receive more than you gave.

While still living in the Northwest, I had one lasting hurtful experience. People can be mean especially out of fear of the unknown or possibly their ignorance. Shelter and protect your person until he or she can manage his or her own situations. After an appointment of my tiring physical therapy, mom needed groceries. She sat me in a chair at the front of a large Albertson's grocery store. It was too hot to leave me waiting in the car. I was sitting out of the way and happy to wait there and rest. I was wearing the black eye patch to retrain my damaged eyes. I held a cane, my scarred head was surgically shaved, I was dressed in sweats, and I was limp with exhaustion from the morning's physical therapy appointment. It was on Sunday; a well dressed, fresh from church older man and his wife approached me. He got near and said quietly and cruelly, "All you need is a monkey and a cup." He then took his pious little wife by the hand, and they strolled away. They were smug and content to have delivered the vicious verbal blow. Attending church on Sunday does not make you a Christian, nor does it make you a decent human being. I was heartbroken; deep inside, I felt the stranger was correct. I was a broken, shamed, miserable wreck. For several days afterward, I refused to get out of the car or let Mom move away from my side in public. Mom returned to collect me on that Sunday morning, and she saw me sitting there crumpled and crying. The hate-filled, old fellow was lucky that she did not find him in the store. Her mama bear instinct had kicked in. She took my cane, and away she went searching for the offenders. I am sure a nasty relocation or use of my long cane at this man's discomfort was her plan.

Most people didn't know what to do when their eyes landed on me and met mine. I was bald and obviously disabled. Many glanced away and quickly averted their faces. It would have been nicer for both of us if they simply had smiled and acknowledged my presence. Everyone counts, and we all have worth. Why not be pleasant?

As I recovered, my back and neck pain stayed constant. Dr. Scott Wood of Wood Chiropractic in Tishomingo, Oklahoma, helped me out of pain; and Scott listened. He took the time to find my source of pain and to carefully make correct life altering adjustments. In the beginning the near fatal Traumatic Brain Injury was foremost, while other deficits had been passed over. With Dr. Wood, overall health was recovered, and my worst pain stopped.

My TMJ joint had been cracked, yet that was not life threatening. A visit to the dentist to remove a cracked molar put additional space in my jaw, allowing it to align. Listen to your loved one; continue searching for assistance to stop any pain. Pain is very tiring and defeating. I was in pain for years. I had migraines, my spine was tight with stress and injury, and my right leg ached.

I fell into the abyss of prescription drug abuse; it is easy to do. I felt totally justified. I used and took advantage of several doctors to gain pain pill prescriptions; I, also, filled and self medicated with my mother's Vicodin and Lortabs. A pain doctor gave me prescriptions for Norco 10-325 mg and morphine. I kept complaining of pain; doctors kept upping the amounts and were willing to write more scripts. I had the nerves in my back burned and steroid injections. I was looking for a medical fix, but the meds weren't working. My life choice of riding and training horses had become too physically hard for me. Alcohol made me incapable and nauseous. I was willingly accepting any medicinal choice, even if it was a dark choice. We had MRI's done and found that there was not significant injury for surgery. After being prescribed and taking morphine while already taking too many Norco tablets, I could not function. The pain doctor said, "I would need alternate medication to wean myself from the drugs. You can't quit on your own." Wrong—I can do anything I desire. I was in pain, but I was destroying my quality of life with the consumption of over 7 Norco 10-325 mg daily for years. I realize the pain doctor was trying to help me; his job is to prescribe drugs and stop pain. The drugs gave me the ability to sleep and to avoid my thoughts and my pain concerns. Yet, I couldn't function; I worked the system and I suffered addiction from my bad choices.

The pain management doctor didn't realize the degree of my stubborn mind. He told me that I couldn't do it without more pills and his help; so, of course, I did. The doctor was correct, it was a terrible few weeks, but not impossible. Mom and I stopped my consumption of pills, and I went cold turkey. The worst symptom was not being able to sleep at night. She and I had a ceremony; we mixed the numerous bottles of pills with warm water and tamped them down a hole in the lower pasture. I had squirreled away over 400 of the Norco 10-325 mg pills. I had more than 40 morphine pills. I was done with being a walking zombie, and I did quit by sheer determination, plus, my mom had helped me destroy my stash. I had no pills left to take even if I had weakened. I have not had anything stouter than Ibuprofen since March 1, 2015. I have since broken my legs multiple times, and I haven't taken any prescription pain medications. I am no longer addicted. I walk daily and try to contain the stress in my life with optimism and love of the Lord. This is my approach. You are free to find whatever works for your loved one. No doubt, a strong, positive mental attitude helps with the stress reduction.

All medication hits me hard and often adversely. I think my traumatized brain has twisted negative reactions to most drugs. I reacted poorly to the CDB Oils and the Medical Marijuana was not helpful, but the opposite. The anti-seizure meds kept me depressed and muddled. Depression and most prescription medication tends to give me suicidal thoughts. Find a competent doctor and receive good advice while checking that your loved one's prescriptions are not battling one another.

Home on the horse training facility suited me best. Animals tend to follow their God given nature. There are few surprises in Mother Nature; she is pure, and she remains

My childhood memories are filled with quiet, serene ranches and cowcamps. I had many God filled locations to ground me.

I have found home is wherever my heart and my mind can find peace. I'm at the top of my mental maturity, and I have made good choices, and I am feeling blessed.

Surround yourself with godly people. Don't be weak or limit your horizons. I did rewrite the list of desirable traits in the people that I now choose to have in my life. In saying godly, I don't mean church-going, self entitled, self righteous people. I don't care if they ever stepped over the threshold of a church. I mean honest, spiritual believers through Jesus Christ knowing God to be the answer. I am speaking of people who maintain a relationship with God. Believers come in all shapes and sizes. Ranchers and old cowboys told us that they were praying for me and continue to pray for me. These kind, stalwart, earthy people have God's ear; God is in them and the Holy Spirit resides in their hearts. I don't discard non believing friends, but love them more. Judging is not our job.

If you are involved in the horse industry, you have probably heard of Tom Dorrance and Ray Hunt. These two men took understanding the motivation of a horse beyond the norm and used the horse's natural inclinations towards a positive goal. As a young horse trainer apprentice, I worked with Mr. Dorrance in Battle Mtn., Nevada, on Tom and Rosita Marvel's huge ranch. He was amazing with his easy comprehension and approach. Both Ray and Tom were some of the first pioneering clinicians willing to market their knowledge with the public and doing it in an easy form to follow; the prior generations held their training secrets close and did not often share except by letting you watch them and figure it out yourself; each horse is different to respond as are humans. I am attempting to share my knowledge to a simple degree that can be mimicked and put to use with humans to strive towards recovery. Tom studied the individual horse and got into the horse's mind. He encouraged the horse to use his natural equine tendencies. As a caregiver, do the same; only you are working with a disabled human. Use your loved one's traits and encourage him or her to wellness and a better attitude by blocking bad behavior, while making the good behavior available. Set up the preferred action to be the easiest course for your loved one to utilize and follow. Think as you work; make adjustments to pull your loved one your direction. Your idea becomes your loved one's idea and their goal without conflict.

You've heard the saying, "The Devil made me do it." This is not funny; it can often be a fact. The Devil is here, and he is busy. If I didn't have faith, I would have nothing. Faith is an unshakeable belief in the Lord God, Almighty. Don't be all self-righteous, and remember it is not our job to judge. A Christian's job is not to fix, but to offer hope through Jesus

Christ. We are all sinners; I love my friends. Some of my dearest friends do not know nor do they believe in God and have a relationship with Him. That is their choice, and I respect the decision; they are my friends forever.

It takes a village to raise a child. It takes a bigger village to repair a Traumatic Brain Injury. A single route and a single person will not alone do the mending. It takes many approaches. Your loved one may need to start over with baby steps. Leave no possibility unopened. It is a unity of diverse elements to find the way. Don't limit your efforts or your accomplishments. Try anything sensible. Be sure to get your loved one involved, included, and working to return.

I was mistaken while at the Elk's Rehab. The medical establishment is correct in saying, "Once a Brain Injury; always a Brain Injury." Possibly do not share this negative thought with your loved one. The truth can hurt when we are too vulnerable to accept it. Your loved one may conclude the possibility of this fact at the right time in their recovery. The Brain Injury upon impact became part of your history and your makeup. I awake every morning with thoughts of my limitations and condition. To see me, I appear normal. Yet, I am changed and altered. Is it harder for me than for other women my age? I do not know, but deep inside, I believe that I have been devalued, so my thoughts do make it a fact. Give life your best shot. Believe every day is a better day.

A TBI's journey is unending. You never ever stop working and traveling towards your destination. Embedded in your mind, you will probably continue to believe, "Once a Brain Injury, always a Brain Injury."

Use your own informed and educated judgment as you proceed to be the caregiver. Sympathetic, well-intentioned people and the public may try to sway you to an easier route. There is no easy route. Both you and your loved one have a surreal, involved recovery pact in play. Don't weaken unless it is a fact that your loved one is too broken to ever recover. I am not saying my way or suggestions are magic. Sadly, some cannot fully recover. Undoubtedly, you have others in your life needing you. You need You. It is going to be hard to find time for everyone. There are no solid answers and no guarantees.

Be prepared, as there will be setbacks and disappointments. My ego, vanity, and sense of sexuality took a beating. It did all get better with time and effort. Not perfect, but better.

Memory with honesty is good. Everyone has past emotional scars, and we all have health scars. Look to your future. Love your good life. Be positive. Be thankful. Be strong. Be kind. Be happy. Just Be. I hope you can understand the concept and "Be" content.

I am typing this on my smart phone at 3:00am

lying in my bed. I awoke with my head full of thought. I cannot wait to put this to paper. If I wait, my thoughts will disappear. My fleeting thoughts fly away if I hold them back or hold them too long.

There remains a party going on in my head, and I don't know all of the noisy revelers. I wish it would stop. We must take control of our lives and our destiny. You learn to take responsibility. My compulsive actions do fall on the Autism spectrum at times. I do have to resist the counting cadence of 0 to 21—breathe—21 to 0—all better now. My brain is in constant flux and spewing information to me, and I decipher it differently than before the TBI.

I was hesitant to honestly share my story, as I fear many of you won't get it. "Once a brain injury, always a brain injury" goes around repeatedly on my memory spool. It is true only as much as we allow our history to paint us. Pick good memories. We all are slaves to our own brain. You be the master of your own destiny and your thoughts.

The documentation and sharing of my true story is another very scary thing. I wrote it down for everyone to see and to judge. I am exhausted by being scared. Fright burns a lot of energy. I doubt "scared" is the persona people see in me. We hide ourselves. Scared is not the best adjective to describe me to the world, but it is the one that stays in my head. Please do not look at me with disdain or superiority.

Be honest with yourself. You are not perfect, and you must know it. None of us are perfect nor are we sinless.

I feared opening my memory gates and sharing. Past incidents and crazy, frightening thoughts might consume my mind if allowed. In the hospital and while I was healing, I saw too many tragic and sad life occurrences. Normally, a person is in his or her twilight years before facing these fears. Reality is fragile. In a second, your place in this world can alter, and it might not alter to the good. Last night, I let fear and worry gain control of my mind. This morning, I said, "Devil get behind me," and he did. I believe that God's love heals me; therefore, it does. Brother Joe Patterson, our beloved pastor at Legacy Pointe Baptist Church in Whitesboro, Texas, gave me this beautiful, promising scripture to consider and to hold. I use this chosen verse when I have lost my confidence and my history of the Traumatic Brain Injury is causing me to doubt myself. Reciting the scripture returns my joy and my confidence. "For God hath not given us the spirit of fear; but of power, and of love, and of a sound mind." II Timothy 1:7

The idea of sharing my inspiring recovery has taken on its own life. I write on autopilot, and I can't walk away. I must get the pertinent facts correct and recorded. I am less afraid, and life is good. I pray that I am not found lacking by my peers. You cannot and will not understand my unusual and tiring mental calisthenics. I hope you never do. The only way to understand is to receive and survive a Traumatic Brain Injury. If you don't live it, you won't get it. Have you read any Stephen King novels? At times, it is as if I am entrenched in one of his stories. I do not like the plot, and I worry about the ending.

I imagine much of the populace has bizarre, unwelcome thoughts and some degree of fright. We live in a complicated, unstable time.

I have the excuse of the severe Traumatic Brain Injury. I hope I do not regret the opening of Pandora's Box hidden within my mind. We are who we perceive ourselves to be. I tell myself, "I am not a weak loser. I am not scared." The goal is to help your lost love one recover his or her life as best as he or she can; with God all things are possible.

I am a winner. I live a blessed life. God is here. God is constant. Thank you for your interest and your consideration. In my heart I know I returned, mentally and physically, due to the love and guidance of others. I was blessed by being on prayer chains across our great Nation; intercessory prayer is powerful.

It was a long trek, and hopefully, it is not nearly over. Every single person struggles every day; disabled or not. We all need to work to better ourselves. The desire in my writing is that my story will guide your loved one to a success story of their own found with the help and the love of their caregivers.

## Our Common Sense Suggestions

These suggestions are not ordered by importance.

The caregiver has the toughest most critical job of helping their loved one return. The caregiver's life will often be put on hold. I was the center of Mom's universe, and she provided what I needed; her strong personality and will forced me to overcome. It is very difficult for some people, but finding and using common sense is a huge element. The caregiver must provide motivation, love, and empathy, and supply human warmth through touch, compassion, encouragement, and sometimes by showing disappointment. When appropriate, showing displeasure at repeated failures and demanding more positive results is the proper response. The caregiver needs to be aware and make measured, intelligent decisions; make thoughtful effort to teach your loved one the difference between acceptable and non-acceptable response by praise, or if needed, applying a measured reprimand to bring the point to his or her attention. Don't over reprimand, but bring it home. A traumatic brain injured person must not be allowed to hide behind his or her injury if it is possible to do better. Remember, every child will push you to your limits!

## 1

**Speak like he or she is your intelligent equal.** Don't be superior. Get on their same level when conversing. It is exhausting to tilt your head up and try to process from the seat of a wheelchair. Allow them to relax their shoulders and relax their mind. I was confused and embarrassed by my plight. My neurosurgeon, Dr. Ronald Jutzy, showed huge kindness and insight; his methods got through the mental and physical limitations and my barriers. At every follow up appointment, Mom would roll my chair into an examining room. Dr. Jutzy would enter the room, happy to see us. He'd bend over, give me a hug, and promptly plop down on the floor in front of my wheelchair. He'd put his hand on my knee and start visiting with me. He didn't talk to me; he talked with me. He got on my physical level. He made me think that he enjoyed this time with me. He didn't hurry and was not dismissive. Dr. Jutzy saw me as a person. Looking back, I believe that Mom helped make this happen. You, as caregiver, supply the doctor insight regarding whom or what your loved one was before the injury. Help him or her see what is missing, and define the pieces of the puzzle that you are hoping to fit back together. This doctor is merely a person, use common sense and kindness when asking for their help and their skills to repair your loved one.

2

**Make attainable goals for your loved one, and applaud every little accomplishment.** The reaching of any goal, may take longer than you expect; do not weaken. When your brain is misfiring, it requires much to accomplish any act. Scratching one's own nose might be a huge pride building event.

3

**Never say never.** Do not squelch recovery enthusiasm. Let them dream of big things and of a return to normalcy in their future. We all need to have dreams. Don't discourage your person. Miracles do happen. You can allow impossible dreams if the dream is causing them to aspire and to be happy. Say, "Not today or not yet, but probably soon. Let's start with an easier goal and get it done."

### 4

Plan frequent rest periods; it is exhausting and fearful to receive too much input. Assist them to recapture their sense of identity and self. **Help them visualize.** Using memories of their old life, paint them a picture using words to encourage growth and positive change.

### 5

**Direct your love one to the best physical shape they are capable of attaining.** Stop and think; if your person is packing extra weight that will make every movement harder and their balance and bodies will suffer. Thin might be beyond them, but strive for the healthiest possible.

### 6

I was and still am very repetitive. The "21" count routine can and sometimes still returns when I am pressured. **Allow mistakes without disdain.** It is hard for me to release most issues and operate on what is considered a correct routine. When my routine is interrupted, I may have to go back to the beginning and restart. A return to the beginning of the conversation thread if I am interrupted is often necessary. I have trouble letting the other person converse. If I wait my turn, my thought might just disappear. I don't mean to be rude; it is often the best that I can do in our conversation.

7

**Keep the emphasis on what they can do,** and stay quiet about what they cannot do. I'm pretty sure they probably know they can't do everything, yet. Work on brain exercises; a strong, exercised mind will start clicking along smoother. Game boys and table games can add to one's dexterity and mental skills. For a long while, the computer screen shining in my face distracted my thoughts. Consider what factors might be confusing. The brain injury victim will take time from the other family members; the hurt person can suck the life out of the world revolving around them. Remember not every person can make a full comeback. Hopefully, hard work and help will cause improvement to their life and to their family. Be reasonable with your expectations. The doctors must answer your questions with medical facts. Not me, I can and I do provide hope, but do not be blind or ignore facts. I truly know there is a worse place than death. I spent time there and wish it on no one.

## 8

Life is made up of choices. I chose to go to the horse show. I chose to ride. My horse fell. I chose to ride him down and had the resulting injury. I could blame no one, not the horse, and not myself; stuff happens. Many support people, especially the parents of the other patients in the rehab hospital, were angry about their circumstance. That is understandable, but get over it. Anger will just keep it festering and make the Brain Injury victim feel guilt, sorrow, and more confusion. It happened. **Never use anger or hate, but fix whatever problem with positive steps.** Don't go backwards. Use small steps, and raise the bar each time for another attainable level. Cultivate their inherent personal hardiness. Thank God and help your loved one be proud to be a survivor. Help them see they are lucky as they are alive and functioning! Take them to see injured children that are in a worse condition than they. Show them in comparison that they are improving and to celebrate; try not to allow them to whine nor linger on their failures. Be careful not to shun them while admonishing.

## 9

I made recovery leaps and then would plateau for a time. It was hard and even harder on the people in my circle. Life rotated completely around my health situation. I was obsessed with it; my health was all I could talk and think about. After leaving the Elk's Rehab, my folks started taking me to a local TBI Support Group. I did not like it. Possibly, the rehab group is just what your loved one needs. It was not for me. These people were injured, yet some of the comments at the large support group made it seem we were all permanently injured. **Do not label anyone with the critical demoralizing title of "Traumatic Brain Injury."** Just because they had one doesn't mean they are nor will they remain a traumatic brain injury. Encourage them to normalcy or as close as they can return. I was back out into the mainstream of life. Life is where I wanted to remain. Attending and listening made me sad, the group leader's comments often made me feel disabled and lacking when I went to their parties and meetings. At my request, we quit going to the brain injury support group. I had to find myself, and I had to become confident in public. Real life and joining the whirling busy world was still too confusing, but give it time. Don't give up; do not be happy with less than your loved one can become without encouraging and making a huge lasting effort.

### 10
**Don't display and take your person out in public places until they are ready; keep them safe.** Remember this is

about them and not about you and your needs. Expect growth and improvement, but never forget that your loved one was injured and needs time, rest, and help to find the will to recover. Don't chauffer them around and make a big dramatic display of assisting them. I am positive, your job for a time is to keep them sheltered. Let them have time to regain their strength and dignity of self before venturing out into the public arena. Sadly, I saw some people using their loved one for attention and to gain sympathy for themselves. If, as a caregiver, you think this fiasco is about you and your feelings, then you need to step aside, now.

### 11

Whenever I looked in any of the faces of my true support group, **I saw success and pride reflected back** in their eyes. As a sick and weakened soul, I chose to believe they knew something. I remember the day that I chose to get well. Mine was a conscious decision made in a less than fully conscious, but hopeful mind.

### 12

I was blessed by my loved ones to help me attain my goals. **They provided the proper stimulus to reach me.** They set me up to get well. I was sick and hurt. My loved ones provided the vehicle and safe environment in which

I traveled. Think about what your loved one needs in life. Then dangle the hope like a carrot or treat in front of them and cheer them towards it.

## 13

One of the things that made me feel hurt and still makes me seriously angry is being the object of laughter. Never let your loved one think you are demeaning them for the fun and humor of it or laughing for any other negative reason. It seems to be a common trait among head injury victims; **don't laugh at us,** unless we are laughing as well!

Dee Dee, the wonderful aide and friend, gave me the daily job at the Rehab of picking out my outfit. She gave me respect and didn't laugh. I worked hard to please her and to gain her respect in return. I fear that I often looked and smelled like a drunken, gaited, mismatched, garish harlot while at the rehab facility. Dee Dee did not laugh; in her opinion no worries. I was evolving, and this wonderful caregiver was allowing my growth.

## 14

**Always follow through and honor your answers and your promises.** If the situation changes and your answer becomes "No", please explain the change. Still today, I process most every comment and incident through a shattered looking glass; I think my deficits create every failure. Please don't leave your loved one hanging in wait; reply in a timely manner and don't cause them to feel neglected or like they are a negative aspect in your life. The Traumatic Brain Injury left me being hypersensitive; consider and address that painful issue by giving closure to each communication or promise. Be kind.

**15**

If possible, your person will reach out and grasp your hand to struggle onward. Don't force them; bait and charm them. Your job is foremost to **Love them.**

During the long, tedious recovery, I considered killing myself on numerous occasions. I have a loaded pistol within reach much of the time. I held and fondled the gun. I did not pull the trigger. I did not lose hope. I was receiving positive help; I had people listening with care and concern. The will to live is huge. God stayed in the room, and He calmed my mind, and He held my hand.

Black and white, right or wrong, win or lose; to me life was all very cut and dried. I did grow up knowing God. Mom saw that my brother and I understood the basic beliefs within the Bible and that we believed The Word. My dad nearly always did the right thing; he was a God fearing man. I've found it to be a clear concept, and my thoughts are simple—know Jesus Christ as your Lord and Savior who died and rose, again. Share the exclusivity of the gospel of Jesus. Ask and accept God into your heart. Through Jesus Christ, God is the Answer. "I am the way, the truth, and the life: no man cometh unto the Father, but by me." St. John 14:6

Do unto others as you want them to do unto you. Most of us are born with an inherent understanding of right versus wrong; live the Ten Commandments. Be able to look yourself in the eye every morning as you gaze in the mirror. If you don't like what you see, ask God for forgiveness and help. God is King; He is the Alpha and the Omega, the Beginning and the End, the Almighty. Be aware the Devil lurks everywhere; his demons are many. Lucifer is waiting for us to make poor choices; deny him. The same freedom of choice that might lead you to an injury or death can lead you to great joy, fellowship, and everlasting life. Christian choices do come back to you. Life is good and God is Great.

*Many applicable suggestions and informative truths to overcome a Traumatic Brain Injury are included in the writings of my honest book. I am reaching out to everyone in every walk of life. Consider my success story for counsel, and intelligently apply the ingredients to help your loved one. God is my constant true anchor. My inspiring journey of hope through Jesus Christ is offered as a blessing to everyone.*

# Acknowledgments

The pages of this book are too few to acknowledge the myriad of people that touched my life in a positive and loving manner. Never doubt that showing you care by reaching out to a friend or a loved one contributes to their recovery; a kind gesture, touch or smile might be monumental to them. My life threatening accident was in 1994, twenty five years later, my life remains blessed with these loving and empathetic people while more good people in my path join the effort to continue bolstering me onward to succeed.

I am indebted to my family, my friends, Dr. Ronald Edwin Jutzy, MD, FAANS and foremost thankful for the grace of God. These people and the Lord helped me gain the return of my mind; with my functioning brain came back my good life.

I have a personal goal throughout this book and in sharing my story. Let us unite, analyze, and create a road map for other brain weary and broken travelers to navigate a return back to their original selves.

Gala Nettles, you are a special blessing, a successful published author and valued friend, you have encouraged me, and your grace filled friendship kept me spurring onward to complete my book and get the message of Hope told. You encouraged me with my writing and propelled me along to tell my story. She is an amazing woman, friend and an accomplished author. Gala, your belief in my ability kept me writing and struggling to reach a higher goal than I thought possible and I thank you from the bottom of my heart.

Thank you to Whitney Finley, copy editor extraordinaire, for her perfect work editing my grammar.

Thank you to each valued and remembered person that did reach out and helpfully force me to return. Every Brain Injury is different and not all can return. I truly believe, with help, nearly every person can improve his or her lot in life. Hope should not be removed until all avenues are explored. If this Cowgirl could return, many others can ride a similar trail. Let us work to make this happen and recognize Traumatic Brain Injury in a different light

# Photography Credits

Thank you to following photographers who have contributed to this book.

J Bar D Photography *pages: 37, 136, 153*
Kathy Bergh Peth *page: 133*
Kat Rodgers *page: 162*
Kathy Skippen *page: 101*
Linda Rosser *page: 127*
Primo Morales Photography *pages: 15, 138*
Red Oar Press *page: cover, 113*
Ross Family *pages: 35, 56, 67, 139*
Robin Ross *pages: 78, 144*
Shannon Slavens *pages: 73, 132*
Vea Loy Ross *pages: 33, 44, 112, 121, 125*
White Digital *page: 131*

*All images were provided by the author from personal records, not the original source.*

TPS 211111

Made in United States
Troutdale, OR
06/24/2025

32360943R00096